DEVELOPMENTAL SEQUENCES OF PERCEPTUAL-MOTOR TASKS

MOVEMENT ACTIVITIES FOR NEUROLOGICALLY AND RETARDED CHILDREN AND YOUTH

BY BRYANT J. CRATTY
ASSOCIATE
UNIVERSITY OF CALIFORNIA
LOS ANGELES

DATE DUE

GAYLORD   PRINTED IN U.S.A.

FOREWORD

Developmental Sequences of Perceptual Motor Tasks represents a major contribution and approach in devising appropriate movement activities for neurologically handicapped and mentally retarded children and youth. Dr. Cratty is unique among physical educators: he is concerned with physical education not only as a means of facilitating motor skills and physical fitness, but also in the fact that he outlines how specific perceptual-motor tasks may enhance the learning process for children with intellectual deficits or learning disorders. Thus he helps identify and bring into perspective certain areas of pupil achievement which challenges the highest order of understanding and skill in the responsibilities shared by special educators and physical education teachers.

One need not adopt or abandon any particular neurophysiological theory in order to accept the practical value of a guide for suggested movement activities arranged in developmental sequences. However, it is important to know that the suggested activities are derived from research and experience with handicapped children. Over the past several years Dr. Cratty has served as a consultant to the Special Education Branch of the Los Angeles City Schools. During this time he conducted or directed several studies and provided demonstrations concerned with the motor development and fitness of handicapped pupils.

This publication was initially written for experimental use in response to specific requests by special educators for a guide that could be employed by teachers of educationally handicapped and mentally retarded pupils. Its early popularity confirmed the need and practicality of such an aid. Other physical education teachers and special educators will also find *Developmental Sequences of Perceptual Motor Tasks* a highly useful reference in their work with handicapped children.

Ernest P. Willenberg
Director of Special Education
Los Angeles City Schools
April 1967

PREFACE

It is the purpose of the text to present selected developmental sequences of perceptual-motor activities which will be helpful in the education of retarded and neurologically handicapped youngsters. The material is written primarily for teachers of special education and for other professional workers concerned with the learning problems of atypical children. In addition it is hoped that certain of the chapters will be helpful to the parents of children with learning problems.

The data upon which much of this material is based were obtained from an investigation directed by the author, involving over 200 retarded and neurologically handicapped children, carried out in Los Angeles County during the summer of 1966 (30). These data aided to determine the approximate order of difficulty for various tasks contained within the sequences of activities presented.

Some clinicians have suggested that perceptual-motor activities constitute magical panaceas for children with mild and severe learning difficulties. The author takes no such position. At the same time it is believed that perceptual-motor activities constitute an important part of the educational program for exceptional children. The retarded seem to learn best by doing; these youngsters improve intellectually when confronted with concrete experiences in which they can participate.

The neurologically handicapped youngster evidences perceptual-motor difficulties which block his intellectual endeavors. Amelioration of these movement problems can usually aid this kind of youngster to realize his potential in the classroom.

Performance in playground skills form an important component of the base from which children judge themselves successful or unsuccessful. Innumerable classroom tasks including writing, typing, reading, and the like involve components of perceptual-motor functioning. Other less obvious components of classroom learning may be enhanced by using gross movement as a learning modality.

It was with the above guidelines in mind that this text was written. Improvement upon the materials contained in its pages will be forthcoming when the findings of additional research, some contemplated, some underway, are available. Evidence relating to the effects of long-term programs of motor activities upon children's emotional, intellectual and motoric functioning is particularly needed.

The approach taken by the author is a rather pragmatic one. Rather than preoccupation with the neurological underpinnings of motor activities, it is suggested that the educator ask himself with what kinds of perceptual-motor activities does the child have difficulty? After this has been established, the educator should then attempt to rectify the deficiencies the child evidences through the application of perceptual-motor sequences carefully graded in difficulty and appropriate to the ability levels the child exhibits. A mentally or neurologically handicapped child learns by doing, and the special educator's is to devise tasks which aid in the amelioration of his learning problems. It is thus desired that the material in this text will aid the teacher to make programs of perceptual-motor activities more meaningful in improving the learning efforts of the children in their charge.

The materials presented are intended to be only illustrative of *some* of the sequences which may be applied to the atypical child. It is not assumed that these tasks represent a complete list of activities. The reader is urged to experiment and modify these procedures as the situation and the individual differences of the participants dictate change.

At the same time it is believed that the broad scope of motor activities are represented on the pages which follow. Activities to enhance balance, body-perception, thinking, ball catching and throwing, agility, locomotor behavior, manual dexterity, and the like should be among the underpinnings of every program of physical education, and of most programs of special education, particularly when the children evidence moderate to severe movement and/or learning problems.

It is believed important, when possible, to document the assumptions made and the techniques presented in the text. The bibliography at the completion of the text may stimulate the reader who is oriented toward a scientific approach to problems of educational methodology to explore further some of the important questions dealing with various relationships between motoric functioning and intellectual endeavor. Perhaps no other area within educational programs for atypical youngsters is more in need of exact experimental clarification.

The author would like to thank innumerable individuals who aided in the collection of data upon which much of the text's material is based. Numerous administrators of various programs for atypical youngsters within the County of Los Angeles have also aided the author to validate some of the assumptions presented by permitting him to institute programs of movement education for children with learning and/or movement difficulties.

Dr. Ernest Willenberg, Director of Special Education for the Los Angeles City Schools, engaged the author as a consultant during the school year 1966-67 and permitted him to apply some of these activities directly to retarded and neurologically handicapped children. Dr. Ivy Mooring, Director, Los Angeles County Mental Retardation Services Board, conceived of the research project which resulted in the collection of much of the data undergirding the text.

Mr. S.N. Johnson of the Special Services Branch of the Los Angeles County Department of Parks and Recreation, and Dr. Donald Handy, Chairman of the Department of Physical Education at the University of California, Los Angeles, sponsored the initial investigation. Mr. Edward Hay, Psychometrist from the Los Angeles City Schools, Mrs. Jean Jordan, Mr. Jerry Porter, Mrs. La Verne Sopp, and Mrs. Ellen Lambell of the Los Angeles County Department of Parks and Recreation helped in the collection of data and in the evaluation of children, many of whom had not previously been considered "testable". Dr. William Hirsch, and Miss Shirley Wolk, principals of schools of special education within the Los Angeles District have aided the author and his students in innumerable ways related to programs of motor education and of research in the schools.

Mrs. Diane Leichfield, Director of Programs for

Mentally Retarded and Multiply Handicapped has also extended to the author her fullest cooperation and support. Dr. Marianne Frostig has also helped the author to see more clearly some of the perceptual-motor relationships defined within the pages of the text. In addition Dr. Frostig has referred numerous children with perceptual-motor problems to the author's program for Movement Education at the University of California at Los Angeles.

The author would also like to thank Mrs. Ruth Amster for her diligence and expertise in the preparation of the illustrations.

The content of the text, however, remains the writer's sole responsibility. Comments from the reader concerning the material presented are eagerly sought.

Bryant J. Cratty

TABLE OF CONTENTS

Page

FOREWORD III

PREFACE. IV

CHAPTER I 1
Introduction

CHAPTER II 4
Perceptual-Motor Characteristics of Mentally Retarded
and Neurologically Handicapped Children and Youth

CHAPTER III. 13
Teaching Guidelines

CHAPTER IV. 19
Perceptions of the Body and of Its Positions in Space

CHAPTER V 25
Balance

CHAPTER VI. 37
Locomotion

CHAPTER VII 44
Agility

CHAPTER VIII 52
Strength, Endurance, Plus Flexibility Equals Fitness

CHAPTER IX. 60
Catching and Throwing Balls

CHAPTER X 66
Manual Abilities

CHAPTER XI. 73
Moving and Thinking

CHAPTER XII 77
Summary and Program Suggestions

GLOSSARY 80

BIBLIOGRAPHY 82

INTRODUCTION

Within recent years educators, experimentalists and clinicians have taken an interest in the use of motor activities in programs of education for retarded and neurologically handicapped children. This emphasis has been prompted by several kinds of observations: (1) Severely and trainable retarded children and youth learn primarily by doing; tasks involving observable movement are apparently the experiences most suited to their basic educational needs (87). (2) Retardates rarely evidence the ability to engage in abstract symbolic thought, so that the main evidence of their thought processes comes in the form of some observable action, either manual skill or more gross activity (24). Thus, by improving their physical skills in a concrete way, they may enhance their ability to function intellectually at increasingly higher levels (87).

Increasing attention has also begun to be paid to the child classified as neurologically handicapped (35) (71). These children with I.Q.'s ranging from about 70 to over 100 evidence mild to moderate perceptual-motor problems which inhibit their classroom functioning and their proficiency in games valued by their peers (30) (50) (53). The chapters which follow contain activities through which these children's perceptual-motor attributes may be improved.

There are indications in recent studies that with improvement in motor skill and fitness the retardate and neurologically handicapped will sometimes begin to perform better in tests of intellect (86). Some researchers have suggested that by achieving competency in motor tasks the child's self-image is enhanced, promoting him to strive harder in a variety of activities both intellectual and physical. The investigations whose findings point to this general effect unfortunately often suffer from too few subjects and/or inadequate statistical treatment of the data (24) (87).

Some clinicians view movement experiences for the retardate and neurologically handicapped as essential tasks through which to enhance his intellect and various perceptual attributes (35). These individuals claim that by "filling in" the steps in a child's basic locomotor development changes within a damaged central nervous system will occur which will enable the child to organize his experiences more efficiently and in a direct way enhance other sensory functions including hearing and seeing (35) (61).

Others make less extravagant claims for motor activities and include a variety of movement tasks in programs designed to improve the capacities of children with learning problems (50) (71). Proponents of this second "school of thought" claim less for motor activities but do propose that perceptual and motor functions are inseparable, and that training in motoric functioning will improve the child's ability to structure, judge, and order events to which he is exposed.

Evaluation of these conflicting theories is made difficult by the lack of "hard" experimental evidence supporting either as well as by certain gaps in knowledge about the complex functioning of the human nervous system. At the same time there is enough reliable information available to make certain generalizations which lead toward a theory which *encompasses* motor activities, yet which does not devote itself exclusively to their use (96).

The statements which follow are, for the most part, based upon a number of research studies which are more than merely clinical descriptions. These statements are the result of analyses of investigations which, because of their clarity, may be replicated. These assumptions are the result of the application of the scientific method problem solving which includes: the clear delineation of a problem; making an educated guess concerning its resolution; collecting data using objective and valid measures; the use of proper controls; and the treatment of the resultant data with acceptable statistical procedures based upon established laws of probability (30) (95). After reading the foregoing, the uninitiated might be led to believe that using the scientific method to discover the "truth" is indeed singular in its direction and methodology. Such, of course, is not the case. Research is never uncontaminated by experimental bias and philosophical speculation, nor should it be. The experimenter philosophically selects the problem for investigation and decides among a number of alternatives how he might structure its solution. Similarly, interpretation of the data and the conclusions arrived at are often subject to a number of interpretations.

In the statements which follow, it has been attempted to delineate major findings on this problem acceptable to a majority of the members of the scientific community interested in human behavior.

1. The motor and intellectual abilities of more severely retarded children are more closely related than are various motor and intellectual measures of children with less severe mental impairment (30) (66) (112).

2. If manual tasks are simple enough and retarded children are given enough time they can many times approach the performance of normals (81). Dividing a complex motor task into parts enhances the retardates' chances of performing it successfully.

3. The fitness of retardates has been demonstrated to be significantly inferior to the fitness of normal children (6) (46). Usually the retardate with this deficiency achieves

scores on fitness tests which are elicited from normal children from two to four years younger in age.

4. Retarded and neurologically handicapped youngsters often exhibit their best motor performance scores in late childhood and early adolescence, from the ages of eleven to thirteen, in contrast to normal children who achieve their best performance in late adolescence and early adulthood, from sixteen to twenty years of age (30) (45) (70).

5. Sex differences in motor performance scores are not as marked among retardates as among normal children (30).

6. It is often difficult to determine whether deficiencies in the motor abilities of retardates are due to specific damage to the motor areas of the brain or are caused by their inability to understand complex verbal directions which usually accompany the administration of motor ability tests, or whether the retardates simply are unable to adopt efficient work methods when deciding how to accomplish a complex motor skill (98).

7. Higher inter-correlations are found between intelligence measures and motor skill performance on simple tasks (i.e. the jump-reach test) than when intelligence scores and the performance of more complex movements are compared (30).

8. About 90% of retarded children, classified as having no specific damage to the motor areas of the brain, exhibit appropriate cross-extension patterns when crawling and walking (30).

9. The most inferior group of retardates, motorically, are children with Down's Syndrome (107). Next, in order, are children classifiable as trainable retardates (I.Q. from 30-50) (30).[1] Children classifiable as educable retar-

---

[1]Throughout the remainder of the text "Trainable Retardates" include children within the I.Q. range mentioned, but exclude children with Down's Syndrome.

dates and educationally handicapped usually produce similar scores and significantly superior to those elicited from trainable retardates (30).

10. In trainable retardates, the quality most highly correlated to overall perceptual-motor abilities, balancing, agility movements, and the like, are scores obtained when the child is asked to identify body parts and his position in relation to objects. Balance seems to be a central factor in the motor ability of children classified as educable retardates and educationally handicapped (30).

Although it is obvious that much additional information needs to be verified via the collection of more exact data, particularly with regard to various training effects of motor activities, the following assumptions underlie much of the information in the chapters which follow.

1. While there is no direct evidence that perceptual-motor activities improve various intellectual functioning (there is no general agreement as to what intellectual ability is), there are *certain components* of the overall educational program to which movement activities can contribute in a positive way. More explicit information relative to enhancing serial memory ability, form perception, and the like are found in the chapters which follow (67) (71).

2. Perception and motion are at times inseparable. As a child moves he has to organize the world visually (113). And while moving he is able to form additional judgments about visual space with which he is surrounded. Catching a ball involves various components both perceptual and motor. Indeed, most so-called motor activities can be calssified as *perceptual-motor* in nature (27). With the exception of the reflex-like withdrawal of the hand from a hot stove, most human actions depend to some degree upon some kind of judgment. Movements themselves form kinesthetic impressions which together with tactile, vestibular and visual information contribute to the early learning of young children, as well as to the more exact delineating of concepts on the part of older individuals.

3. There is a good deal of direct and indirect evidence that suggests that movement does not necessarily underlie all the thinking processes of all people (1). Adults and children mentally manipulate their environment, and for hours can sit quietly in classrooms acquiring concepts independent of their capacities for action (38) (60). The severely handicapped child with cerebral palsy has been found to have acquired most of the concepts understood by a normal child, despite his inability to move with accuracy or with control (1).

4. The motor and intellectual performances of retardates, while not as specific as in normals, requires careful analysis in order to formulate meaningful and helpful educational programs. Thus on the pages which follow, the programs are based upon an analysis of the characteristics of various groups of retardates and the neurologically handicapped (30).

5. Improvement of a child's general feelings about himself by raising his aspiration level through the enhancement of his motor functioning is justifiable in itself, disregarding any direct relationships between movement and thinking (68) (87) (108) (117) (120).

It is thus concluded that participation in various perceptual-motor activities have a definite place in the total educational program of retarded and neurologically handicapped children, and indeed in the programs of "normal" children. The manner in which they can contribute to this program is specified in the pages which follow.

CHAPTER II
PERCEPTUAL-MOTOR CHARACTERISTICS
OF MENTALLY RETARDED AND NEUROLOGICALLY
HANDICAPPED CHILDREN AND YOUTH

When constructing educational programs intended to improve a desirable set of attributes, it is a frequent practice to simply "try something" and then attempt an evaluation of "what worked." It is the viewpoint of this writer, however, that effective educational programs must be constructed by first deciding upon the behaviors it is desired to improve, and then, measuring these attributes (30). The next step then would be to devise activities which seem to contribute to qualities which are found to be deficient in the population with whom the educator is concerned. The final step should be a second evaluation of the participants in the program to determine whether real change has been elicited. Thus it is believed that in reality programs can only be evaluated indirectly by assessing behavioral change.

To many persons, retarded children are considered similar. However, professional workers and parents of retarates usually make fine distinctions between the conditions contributing to a given kind of intellectual impairment, and to the degree to which a child is mentally handicapped. Thus, children with learning difficulties may be classified on a continuum, based upon scores from mental tests, rather than neatly classified into rather exact niches.

At the same time, it is helpful to deal with various classifications of retardates when describing their attributes. To attempt to describe and classify all children based upon individual clinical inspections would result in a text many times this size.

Thus on the pages which follow, four classifications of children will be discussed: the trainable retardate, the child with Down's Syndrome, the educable retardate, and the educationally handicapped child. The trainable retardate is considered to be a child with an I.Q. of under 50, while the educable retardate has an I.Q. ranging from 50 to 70. The mongoloid child is well known by his appearance and is the result of certain chromosomal aberrations. Benda and others have described this syndrome in more detail than will be attempted here.[1] The educationally handicapped child is attracting increasing attention among special educators and other professional workers within recent years. This child, with moderate to mild brain damage, minimally neurologically handicapped, evidences behavior which evidences varying degrees of both mental and/or perceptual-motor dysfunction (9) (33) (50) (53) (71).

Down's Syndrome. In the 1800's the unusual appearance of mongoloid children seemed to distract experimenters from acquiring deeper understandings of their condition. It was originally assumed that they were the result of some "maverick" gene contributed by an early Asian ancestor. More recent and enlightened investigation of this syndrome has uncovered the fact that the mongoloids are truly "living mutations," usually resulting from a trisomy of the 21st chromosome. Their impairments are "stamped-in" genetically at about the fifth week after conception, and their neurological and biochemical make-up precludes most of them from ever reaching normalcy in perceptual-motor and intellectual functioning.

In addition to a nervous system which usually never fully matures, other characteristics of their endocrine system result in marked obesity after the age of three and one-half

---

[1]Benda, Clemens E., The Child With Mongolism, New York: Grune & Stratton, 1960.

years. Seventy-five percent of these youngsters are said to have some kind of structural abnormality in their cardio-respiratory system. Thus, the severe problems they have when attempting to move with force, efficiency, and speed are understandable (95).

Although the foregoing picture would seem to be a rather pessimistic one, the author has become aware of several of these children who have greatly benefited from intensive perceptual-motor training. While it is desirable to attempt to initiate this kind of training at a rather early age, it is believed that reasonable improvement can be elicited in these children's perceptual-motor functioning.

It is apparent to even the most casual observer that these children have severe movement problems (30). Several scales of motoric maturation against which they have been compared show that many evidence performance expected of normal children of about 3 to 5 years of age (64) (107) even in adolescence.

Body-Image. Body-image ratings are usually based upon the scores of tasks desired to evaluate an accurate concept of the body, its surfaces, and its limbs, as well as its left-right dimensions. Additionally, some batteries of this nature contain tasks through which it is intended to evaluate whether a child can accurately make various perceptual-judgments about other peoples' bodies, and whether the child knows where he is located relative to another object. While relatively little work has been carried out concerning the mongoloid child, the following information represents a survey from the available data (30).

Most of the mongoloids can identify the front, back, and sides of their bodies. At the same time relatively few, about ten percent, can consistently and accurately identify various left-right dimensions of their bodies and limbs. Difficulty is also noted when these children are asked to place themselves relative to objects, *i.e.* "place your left side toward the box." Only about twenty percent of the mongoloids recently evaluated by the author could correctly position their bodies to an object (30).

The abilities reflected in these kinds of perceptual tasks undergo the most improvement between the ages of thirteen and sixteen years. Prior to the early teens these children should be subjected to extensive training if they are ever to make various left-right discriminations relative to their own bodies or to various environmental objects.

Scores on these tasks evaluating body image are highly related to the total perceptual-motor functioning of mongoloids. Scores on certain tests of agility, of hand-eye coordination, and of similar tasks can be predicted with remarkable accuracy upon knowing how well the mongoloid can identify his body parts and make the other perceptual discriminations described above. If only a single type of perceptual-motor training activity could be engaged in by these children, it would seem to be most beneficial to have this training consist of activities which attempt to enhance their body-image.

Balance. The mongoloid child is the least favored motorically of all the groups of retardants discussed on these pages. A large portion of his inability to move well can be attributed to the severe difficulty he has maintaining his balance when walking or engaging in other motor tasks requiring satisfactory equilibrium (30) (107).

In a recent cross-sectional survey of mongoloid children, the balancing ability of youths in early adulthood was only slightly better than that evidenced by children between five and eight years of age (30). About seventy-five percent of mongoloid children cannot stand on one leg for more than a few seconds, while the ability to balance on one foot without vision is often completely absent. Considerable problems are encountered when the mongoloid is asked to engage in moving balance tasks, walking a line, or a wide balance beam.

If a mongoloid child is asked to kneel on both knees, he frequently will fall forward catching himself in a four-point balance on both his hands also. It is thus clear that balance training for the mongoloid is a necessity. There is a considerable amount of experimental evidence to the effect that postural imbalances contribute negatively to perceptual judgments involving the proper alignment of lines in a space field (58) (119).

Balance training for mongoloids would seem an important requisite prior to attempting any more complex perceptual tasks requisite to reading. It seems clear that this training should first be carried out on mats, as the child is asked to assume various four- and three-point balances using his hands and knees in various combinations and in various positions (see sequence #1 chapter 4).

Agility. The majority of the mongoloid children above the age of five years walk and crawl with reasonably efficient cross-extension patterns (30). About fifty percent of these children can jump one or more times using both feet simultaneously. They may be expected to encounter great difficulty, however, if they are asked to hop on one foot; only about one-fourth can be expected to do so. Similarly, only about one-fourth can be expected to jump backwards. Their excess weight is a further handicap when asked to engage in basic agility movements. Simply getting up from a lying to a standing position gives the child with Down's Syndrome considerable trouble. If lying on their backs, for example, and requested to rise, most of the mongoloids can be expected to first roll to their stomachs and then to utilize their arms when ascending as would be expected of a normal child of two to three years of age (30).

The most severe impairment is noted in the perceptual-motor functioning of mongoloids when they attempt to jump, hop, or to otherwise perform some agility movement

with any accuracy. They are almost totally unable to pair gross movements of their bodies with vision with any efficiency. The need for training in simple visual-motor coordinations is apparent if one observes a mongoloid child attempting to jump forwards, sideways, or backwards over a line (30).

The available data make it clear that an educator must start at extremely basic levels when attempting to improve the agility of a mongoloid child. The mongoloid's lack of endurance makes prolonged training difficult for him, a further impediment to his improvement in these qualities.

Throwing and Catching Balls. The author has observed and evaluated several mongoloid children who have acquired remarkable abilities to throw and catch balls. These children, while unable to perform some of the simple agility movements mentioned on the previous pages, were able to shoot a basketball accurately several feet away from the basket and to catch and throw rather small footballs. While these few children are the exception rather than the rule, it is apparent that with training, considerable improvement can be elicited in the performances of these children. The children described above had been given extensive training by physical educators and parents in these skills, but at the same time they had apparently neglected the training of the more basic motor tasks involving simple balance and agility.

Most mongoloid children can catch a regulation air-filled playground ball bounced to them from a short distance away. Only a relatively few, about 10%, however, can be expected to catch balls smaller than 12 inches in diameter. Their brief and unhappy experiences with balls ("they hurt you when they hit you") have encouraged many of these children to avoid these punishing missiles.

The majority of mongoloid children throw with a two-handed overhead motion similar to the throwing patterns of two- and three-year-old "normals." At times, however, after extensive practice, this throwing may be remarkably accurate. About one-fourth can be expected to play a reasonable game of catch and to return the ball within the relative proximity of the child or adult with whom they are playing (30).

Throwing behavior and accuracy remains relatively fixed in mongoloid children as they grow older. However, the ability to catch a ball evidences regular improvement with age. By late adolescence, if given sufficient practice, many mongoloid children can become reasonably proficient if the ball is not thrown too rapidly and/or if the ball is not too hard.

Games. The I.Q. of a typical child with Down's Syndrome hovers around 50. Needless to say, games must be kept at a relatively simple level. The mongoloid child, although traditionally assigned a "sunny disposition" by most clinicians, can become frustrated and hostile if he is repeatedly placed in game situations which require judgments he is incapable of making. He is able to function socially in games with one to three other children, if they are not moving too rapidly and do not contribute to his problems by calling attention to his ineptitudes. The usually socially outgoing mongoloid delights in group activities, and these should be encouraged whenever feasible, preferably with children of similar mental and motor capacities.

Trainable Retardate. The trainable retardate's movement problems are not as severe as those possessed by children with Down's Syndrome. At the same time they are significantly inferior to the educable retardate in most tests of perceptual-motor ability. The degree to which improvement can be expected by a trainable retardate in a motor task depends to a great deal upon the complexity of the task. Similar to the child with Down's Syndrome, the TMR is unfit. His unfitness usually stems from a lack of partici-

pation rather than from innate biochemical problems. He does not participate often; therefore fails to develop the capacity to participate with vigor (65).

Body-Image. The typical TMR seems to have no concept of left and right and will fail to identify correctly his left or right sides, hands, and body position as related to an object. The majority of trainable retardants, however, can correctly identify the fronts and backs of their bodies (30).

The TMR's scores on motor tasks are nearly identical to those elicited by Landon-Down's "unfinished children" in tasks in which they are asked to place their bodies relative to objects. For example, while lying down only about one-fourth can locate their feet nearest a given end of a mat correctly.

In tests of body perception the TMR of ten years thus will evidence the ability of a normal child slightly above the age of four years, while the mongoloid of ten will produce scores expected of normal children below the age of four years. TMR's thirteen and older seem to be significantly more aware of their body and its position in space than TMR's below this age (30).

It would seem that training in these kinds of perceptions would be basic to the acquisition of more complex motor and intellectual skills. For if the TMR does not appear to know where he is and what he is doing, how can one expect him to engage in more sophisticated activities within the educational environment?

Balance. The balancing ability of most TMR's, while not as good as that of the educable retardate, is from one to three years in advance of the mongoloid child. At times the evaluation of balancing ability is "corrupted" by the retardate's adopting inappropriate work methods. When asked to balance on one foot, for example, some TMR's, if not instructed properly, will stand with their legs wide apart while attempting unsuccessfully to lift one limb off the ground (30).

About two-thirds of TMR's can balance for more than five seconds on one foot without vision. At the same time their static and dynamic balancing ability is from four to five years below that of a normal child.

The balancing training for TMR's would be beneficial if at first only four- and three-point balance problems on mats were utilized. Later more complex tasks involving erect balance both in tasks requiring movement (balance beam walking) as well as in static tasks (posturing on one foot) might be employed.

Agility. The vast majority (over 80%) of trainable retardates evidence good cross-extension patterns in their gait and when asked to crawl in unstructured tasks. Over 50% can jump while about 40% can usually hop on one foot several times in succession. Similarly about 40% of TMR children can jump backwards when asked to do so.

Considerable difficulty is noted, however, when these children are asked to hop and jump (both forward and backward) with some degree of visual control. Jumping into squares or over lines, for example, is difficult for all but about 10% of these youngsters, while hopping with any accuracy is difficult for all but about 5%. The social implications of the latter statistic, as a TMR girl attempts to learn hopscotch, is apparent (30).

When asked to arise quickly from a back-lying position the TMR will usually get up without first turning to his stomach. And in general he evidences agility which is more mature in appearance than the child with Down's Syndrome. In many educational and recreational settings, however, it is not unusual to find groups of mongoloids with other trainable retardates not evidencing Down's Syndrome. While the former are of course more severely handicapped motorically, both groups can often be worked with at the same time similar activities (30).

The TMR's "superior" agility can largely be attributed to his usually normal weight. At the same time his unfit muscular system will prevent him from evidencing quick and accurate movements (91).

Throwing and Catching Balls. The trainable retardate also evidences abilities superior to that of the mongoloid when asked to throw and to catch balls. He is usually about one year advanced in these attributes, as compared to the skill of the mongoloid of similar age. At the same time he is deficient when compared to educable retardates and the educationally handicapped. While he is usually able to catch a large softball bounced to him, the vast majority cannot be expected to catch a ball the size of a softball thrown with medium velocity.

The throwing behavior is usually not the infantile two-hand movement exhibited by the mongoloid, but only about forty percent can throw a ball with one hand, and only an extremely small percent will exhibit an appropriate weight shift and step with the foot opposite to that of the throwing arm. The TMR also has difficulty throwing for accuracy. In a recent investigation only about one-fourth could hit a large mat with a playground ball while throwing from a distance of fifteen feet.

So while it seems that trainable retardates can, to some degree, throw and catch balls they do so with considerable difficulty and at a skill level considerably below that expected for normal children of the same chronological age. The most improvement in ball skills seems to occur between the ages of sixteen and twenty years. Their skill in throwing is relatively difficult to train and their ability to track and to catch balls can be expected to evidence regular improvement with age.

Games. It is obvious that the complexities of games engaged in by "normals" would prove traumatic for a TMR. At the same time, it is apparent that the TMR, similar to the mongoloid, enjoys the interactions while at play, if social punishment from his peers is absent.

Similarly it is obvious that any game undertaken·of even a moderate degree of complexity must be carefully prepared for. For example, his laterality problems would make it predicticable that he is as likely to run to first base as he is to head for third base in a game of this nature. Thus prior to attempting a complex base game, he must be carefully introduced to the location and nature of the diamond and, perhaps, be started on a triangular-shaped "diamond" on which the chance of "getting lost" is less likely.

There is an ever-increasing number of studies which suggest that significant improvement in the mental and social functioning of the TMR can be elicited by regular participation in group games. It is believed that this is an important means through which educators may work toward the formation of more complex judgments by these children.

Educable Retardates. The educable retardate, while less fit and adept than the normal child, is significantly superior to the trainable retardate in the performance of most motor tasks (30). Whether this difference stems from an increased ability to organize the verbal directions usually accompanying such tests, or the ability to organize visually the accompanying demonstrations better is difficult to determine. In any case the available evidence indicates that in attempting to improve the perceptual-motor functioning of the educable retardate, he should be separated from the trainable retardate and from the child with Down's Syndrome whenever possible.

It is important to note that in a recent investigation by the author the educable retardate evidenced his best scores in motor tasks between the ages of eleven and fourteen years. After that age his performance seemed to decline (30). In contrast the child who is not mentally impaired evidences his optimum in physical performance in late adolescence and early adulthood (45).

This finding would seem to indicate that the educable retardate, possessing enough intellect to accurately assess his deficiencies, tends to withdraw from physical activity several years earlier than does the normal child. This withdrawal sets in motion a failure-incapacity cycle; less participation results in less capacity when results in less participation, etc. Any training program for these children, therefore, should keep in mind that they need solvable motor tasks in which they can experience success, in order to reverse this "failure syndrome."

Body-Image. Virtually all educable retardates can identify the gross surfaces of their bodies, their sides, backs, and fronts. Similarly over 50% can identify their left and rights, but less than 50% can accurately place their left or right sides nearest objects, or conversely can determine when an object is at their left or right. Two-thirds of these children have difficulty following more complex directions involving the identification of body parts (*i.e.* touch your left knee with your right hand). It is possible, however, that this latter finding may be due to the inability to remember a two-part direction, rather than a lack of awareness of the body parts involved.

At the same time, it would be expected that by chance 50% of a given group would accurately "raise their left hand when asked to do so." So that, as a group, the educable retardates evidence the same apparent lack of awareness of the left-right dimensions of the body as do their less gifted classmates. It has been hypothesized that normal children will usually be successful in making these left-right discriminations at about the age of six years.

Balance. About 70% of educable retarded children can balance on one foot for five seconds with their arms folded across their chest. About 50% can balance for a similar period on one foot with their eyes closed. At the same time an average child of ten years with an I.Q. of from 50 to

70 evidences balancing ability of about a seven-year-old with an I.Q. of 100.

In a recent investigation carried out by the author, test scores in tasks evaluating balance were found to be most predictive of scores elicited from educable retardate on other tasks evaluating agility, hand-eye coordination, throwing, and similar attributes. Thus it is indicated that if a single type of perceptual-motor activity is to be included in a program for educable retardates, tasks intended to enhance balance would be those most welcome. Balance improves most significantly in EMR's between the ages of eight and fourteen years (30).

Agility. The educable retardate can usually hop and jump forwards and backwards three or four times in succession if no degree of accuracy is required. Similarly, almost all educable retardates, if no diagnosed motor problems are present, can walk and crawl with an appropriate cross-extension pattern.

Only from 30 to 50%, however, can be expected to hop and jump *with accuracy*. If tasks similar to hop-scotch are utilized, at least one-half of all educable retarded children can be expected to have considerable difficulty. Jumping backwards with accuracy can be expected to give this group the most difficulty; and more than twice as many can usually be found who can hop forward on one foot as can jump backwards using both feet at the same time!

The majority of educable retardates can get up and down on a mat with reasonable speed and facility. About sixty percent are able to rise from a back-lying position to a standing position within two seconds. However, a normal child can, when asked to do so as "rapidly as possible," can arise in about one second.

Throwing and Catching. While virtually all educable retardates will evidence a cross-extension pattern when crawling or walking, only about one-fourth evidence an appropriate arm-leg opposition when throwing a ball. The majority, when throwing with one hand, fail to shift their weight appropriately during the throw, nor do they take a step with the foot opposite to that of the throwing arm.

Their ability to throw with accuracy, while superior to that of the TMR, is inferior by about two years to that of the normal child. They are usually able to catch large balls bounced to them; however, about 50% of most groups of educable retarded children will be unable to handle small balls in throwing and catching games.

Games. The educable retardate in an inappropriate play situation (*i.e.* with normals) will experience rather severe frustration at his incapabilities. He will usually withdraw or otherwise engage in some kind of compensatory behavior (*i.e.* childishness, hostility, etc.). However, if he is introduced to these gradually, the educable retardate can learn games with reasonably complex rules.

"Success at play" should be the keynote of directors of programs for educable retardates. Participation without apparent success, as has been outlined, will elicit withdrawl and further social and motor impediments.

Neurologically Handicapped Children. By definition the neurologically handicapped child has motor deficiencies. Therefore one should not be surprised to find that he is usually deficient to the normal by about two to three years in most skills. In general his motor profile parallels that of the educable retardate. Care should be taken, however, not to place educables and the neurologically handicapped in the same competitive groups. The neurologically handicapped child is often beset with perceptual inadequacies relatively independent of an average or above average ability to engage in abstract thinking. To place such a child who is accurately aware of his perceptual-motor difficulties into a group of children whose problems are so obviously different will only compound his emotional problems.

Body-Image. The neurologically handicapped child, without exception, has the ability to identify the plane surfaces of his body; however, only about one-third can be expected to correctly identify the body's left-right dimensions. In this respect, they are inferior to the educable retardate. Less than one-fourth can cross their body when requested to make accurate movements, *i.e.* "touch your left shoulder with your right hand."

Balance. The neurologically handicapped child is also inferior to the educable retardate in his ability to balance. An educable retardate of ten years evidences the balance ability of a six-and-one-half-year-old, whereas the neurologically handicapped child of ten years balances as one would expect a five-and-one-half-year-old to do! Impaired balance seems to be a central factor causing the neurologically handicapped to perform poorly in a number of motor tasks.

About one-half have difficulty when attempting to balance on one foot with their eyes closed for more than five seconds. While at the same time they have difficulty in balance tasks requiring accuracy while moving along beams of various widths.

Agility. One-third of the neurologically handicapped children can be expected to evidence an appropriate cross-extension pattern when crawling and walking. This percentage is the largest of any of the groups described in these pages. Many children evaluated as neurologically handicapped are also diagnosable as having mild cerebral palsy, so that this inability to integrate a cross-extension pattern into basic gait requirements is to be expected.

Some of the neurologically handicapped children can hop on one foot better than they can jump from two! This may be due to the fact that one side of their body fails to function well, so that by lifting the "involved" foot from the ground when hopping they can do it better than when dragging it in a jumping task.

The majority, however, cannot hop three or four times on a preferred foot. And only about one-half can jump forwards or backwards three or four times in succession.

When jumping and hopping are required with any degree of visual control, *i.e.* over lines, into squares, etc., only about one-fourth of all neurologically handicapped youngsters are able to do so. The overall agility of neurologically handicapped children is about two to four years deficient when compared to that of normals. The most improvement in general agility can be expected to take place between the ages of eight years and ten years.

It is obvious, just as it is apparent when studying the attributes of the other sub-groups discussed, that the pairing of vision with movement proves a difficult undertaking for most of these children. Thus activities in which the child is merely asked to move, to crawl, etc., would not seem as appropriate as motor skills in which some visual monitoring is necessary.

Agility activities, not involving locomotor activity, are not as difficult for the neurologically handicapped child. Over one-half can rise from their backs to a standing position in one second, while most can accomplish this in two seconds.

Throwing and Catching. The neurologically handicapped youngster is about two years in arrears of the normal child in tasks involving the ability to catch balls. At the same time he usually fails to evidence the ability to throw a ball in an appropriate cross-extension pattern, *i.e.* transferring his weight on the correct foot as he releases the ball.

While about 67% of all educable retardates evidence a cross-extension pattern in their crawling and walking behaviors, only about one-fourth can transfer this general pattern to a throwing task.

Throwing accuracy, involving a target, is also difficult for the neurologically handicapped child. Only about one-fourth can be expected to play a reasonable game of catch, using even a large ball, with a partner fifteen feet away.

Games. Similar to the educable retardate, the neurologically handicapped youngster's abilities tend to "peak" during late childhood rather than during late adolescence as in the case of normal boys and girls. This points again to the necessity of providing motivating and successful activities in social situations which are not threatening to him. The neurologically handicapped youngster can organize more complex rules than can the educable retardate, but his capacities for movement are less than those of the EMR.

Thus it is frequent to see pronounced "emotional overtones" to the performance of the neurologically handicapped youth. His feelings about his performance produce inappropriate muscular tensions which further impede performance, and thus another undesirable circle of circumstances arises; preceived ineptitude, a rise in residual muscular tensions, further ineptitude, preceived ineptitude, withdrawl from activity, decreased capacities, etc. It is up to the educator to be sensitive to this "circle of failure," and to attempt to "break" into it whenever possible with chances for success.

SUMMARY

Educable retardates and the neurologically handicapped are significantly superior to the trainable retardate in perceptual-motor abilities surveyed in this chapter. At the same time the child with Down's Syndrome is, without exception, inferior to other trainable retardates in all physical traits.

Body-perception and spatial relationships involving the body's relationships to objects is a central factor in the perceptual-motor attributes of the more severely retarded children. Similarly balance seems to be a central factor in the complex of attributes possessed by the educable retardate and the neurologically handicapped youngster.

Children with mild to moderate mental and motor impairment, the EMR and the neurologically handicapped child, seem to stop improving as they reach late childhood and early adolescence, whereas the children with less awareness of their relationships between their abilities to that of normals (TMR's and Mongoloids) seem to improve with age up to late adolescence.

Educators dealing with retarded and neurologically handicapped youngsters should, when possible, take this survey of attributes into consideration, and should not place children with dissimilar motoric attributes together for training. The differences in abilities outlined here imply specific programs for each of these groups of children. Suggested schedules and program content are found in Chapter XII.

CHAPTER III
TEACHING GUIDELINES

A discussion of teaching methods appropriate for the motor education of the retarded and neurologically handicapped should stem from a study of their characteristics. For example, as the retarded child is frequently unable to understand and to manipulate abstractions, teaching must be carried out in concrete terms. Demonstrating and, at times, manually guiding movements are usually more appropriate teaching techniques than presenting complex verbal descriptions of the activity.

Formulating a teaching methodology for the teaching of the retardate to perform well physically is somewhat difficult because no sound methodology has been thus far formulated for teaching the *normal* to perform motorically (84). For teaching methology to achieve the best effects it must depend upon an exact analysis of the skills to be taught, the nature of the learner, characteristics of the learning environment, as well as the capacities and potentialities of the teacher himself (26) (72). Too often it is heard that the physical education teacher of the retarded must somehow "slow his teaching down" when dealing with those less gifted mentally; that essentially, the differences lie only in the degree of difficulty of presentation. As a result the few words usually devoted to teaching methodology in discussions similar to this one refer only to the obvious fact that when dealing with retardates a skill must be broken down into its simplest components.

However, the briefest of surveys of the material in Chapter II should reveal that there are real and important principles to consider when attempting to deal with the motor development of retarded and neurologically handicapped children and youth. The material which follows is divided into several sections, one dealing with motivational problems, a second with the nature of the teacher's presentation of material, a third with the timing of the practice schedule, while a fourth covers information concerned with the amount of control to be exerted by the teacher over his charges.

Underlying this material are several assumptions. (a) The teacher of retarded and neurologically handicapped children must be more proficient in analysis of skilled movement than a teacher of "normals." (b) The teacher of retardates should be well oriented in the causes and characteristics of various subclassifications of retardation and causes of motor ineptitude. (c) The teacher of children with learning problems should be an individual who is relatively secure and who can focus his attention upon the needs of the children rather than upon his own needs for status and/or quick success. (d) The physical education teacher of retarded and neurologically handicapped children should be well versed in the components of their total educational setting so that his may complement rather than conflict with other facets of the program.

Communication and Perceptual-Input. Some researchers and clinicians have purported to identify various perceptual-types, individuals who habitually utilize visual, verbal, and/or movement cues when learning (27). These same social scientists have yet to devise a quick and manageable technique which would allow a teacher to quickly assess the manner in which the students in their charge might best be contacted.

It is thus recommended for teachers of all children, and particularly for those of the retarded, that they become proficient in presenting simple verbal descriptions of the hoped-for skill, and also in staging meaningful demonstrations, as well as in manually manipulating their charges. Most normals and probably retardates also utilize more than one type of sensory input when constructing experience, and the types of input depended upon when learning one skill may change when they are confronted with a second task (26) (42) (123).

At times the teacher of physical education may observe a response delay, as the child becomes immobile for a period of time while attempting to organize verbal and/or visual demonstrations into meaningful supports for action. Thus an over-reliance upon the quickest and easiest method possible may interfere with the child's important attempts to integrate input with output.

Recent investigations consistently point to the fact that retarded children seem to retain a memory of the components of pictures which have been visually inspected, for longer periods of time than do normal children! (102) This "eidetic memory" which seems highly developed in retardates should be exploited by the teacher of physical education in the form of complete and detailed demonstrations and films of the activities to be learned.

Several explanations have been advanced for this, *i.e.* that an impaired cortex taking longer to process information obtained visually thus takes longer to dissipate such memories; or, retarded children do not select the central parts of their environment to deal with, paying attention to objects in the background of their space field, thus leading to higher scores on tests of visual retention.

Motivation. Motives may be said to be "things" or circumstances which explain why people *select* an activity or course of action, why people *sustain* their interest in an activity, and/or why individuals work at given levels of *intensity*. It is obvious that a sensitive teacher of children with learning difficulties should give his attention to motivational principles.

Reinforcement is another name given to immediate or long-term rewards for performance. Some learning theorists claim that no learning occurs without some kind of reinforcement present in the learning situation. Numerous studies have documented the fact that rather subtle gestures and utterances by a teacher can prove motivating. Similarly investigations have also documented the fact that continued and regular reinforcement tends to "wear off." Irregular reinforcement schedules have been found at times to elicit more vigorous activity on the part of both human and animal subjects (31) (72) (82) (89).

Ignoring this latter finding, many teachers constantly and continually offer their approval in the form of a fixed smile or a phonograph-record-like "that's good!" as the retardate performs (109). It would seem that a more effective course of action would be to offer support and encouragement as often as necessary, but to reward by sounds denoting approval only when the child does well and exceeds his past efforts. It must be remembered, however, that improvement of children with neuromotor problems usually consists of extremely small steps forward, and the teacher should be sensitive to the acquisition of these. For example, merely looking at a manual skill task on a table top for a few seconds may constitute improvement by a severely retarded child (as contrasted to not looking at it), and thus should be rewarded with sounds of approval. On the other hand these same words of approval should not be forthcoming the following day unless the child begins to deal overtly with the task at hand, if only for a few seconds.

Research indicates that unspecific verbal encouragement by a teacher has not the same effect as encouragement accompanied by the statement of reasonable goals (108) (120). The teacher should continually aid the retarded and neurologically handicapped child to formulate achievable goals.

One of the more important classifications of motives are those intrinsic to the task. Well documented studies with primates and children attest to the innate classifications of motives variously termed curiosity, manipulatory drive, or exploratory behavior. These drivers are usually elicited when the task is novel to the learner, and represents an optimum degree of complexity thus challenging him to display and exercise his capacities for movement (82) (108).

It has been found that there is an optimum degree of task novelty and/or complexity inherent in a given task on a given day which will elicit the most interest on the part of a child. In the case of normals this degree of complexity is relatively broad. A normal child, if the task is perceived as difficult, depending upon his age, will usually focus his attention on it for a period of time and incur various degrees of frustration while attempting to master it. On the other hand if the normal, particularly in a group situation, is bored by the simplicity of the task, he will usually "bear with it" and "go along with the group," realizing that all group members are not as gifted as he.

Retarded or neurologically handicapped youngsters, on the other hand, will not often tolerate such a broad spectrum of complexity when attempting to deal with tasks. They will quickly reject, and otherwise evidence avoidance behavior, when confronted with a task which is seen as too difficult and threatening or may become insulted if the task is perceived as too easy and beneath their preceived capacities (33) (53). Furthermore, the retardate's perceptions of novelty and complexity of tasks fluctuates daily. The implication of this should be obvious to the teacher. He must devise several different ways of eliciting the same motor response in retardates, methods which present increasingly complex problems to be mastered, but do not prove too difficult by attempting to "jump" too large an "ability gap." In failing to accommodate to this principle the teacher will lose one of the most effective motivational tools, the basic human need to master a task through the exercise of the capacity for movement (12) (78) (108) (120).

The "Drainage Theory" of Physical Activity. For decades one of the primary justifications for physical activity within the normal school setting was that it somehow drained off destructive energies which interfered with the "true" job of the school, *i.e.* thinking. While this initial premise has been largely unsupported by experimental evidence, application of these assumptions to the teaching of retarded and neurologically handicapped children is fraught with peril.

To attempt to somehow "relax" the hyperactive retardate by "drawing off" his energies through vigorous and rapid physical activity and exercises usually has the reverse effect (33). The retardant becomes more excitable if he is aroused with an excess of motor activity. The retardate should be given experiences which help him to place himself under control, not activities which simply serve to arouse him and make his self-control and his control by others more difficult (80).

Retardates and neurologically handicapped youngsters should be emotionally aroused through physical activity only when they have proved themselves capable of doing so without excess excitability occuring. While certain types of retardates, distinguished by their consistent lethargic behavior, can be aroused in a constructive manner in games and other motoric endeavors, the physical educator should proceed with caution when attempting to "drain excess energies" by engaging in hard "workouts." (74)

Practice Schedule. It is an often stated fact that spaced practice elicits more and quicker improvement than practicing for prolonged periods of time on a single motor task. This is probably more true in the case of retardates than when normals attempt to master motor skills. At the same time it must be remembered that if the task is not boring to the mentally deficient child and his attention is obviously focused upon it, to remove him from his work simply to satisfy a teaching "principle" would be folly (69) (73) (91).

The physical education teacher of children with learning problems should usually plan a greater variety of activities within a given time period than he would plan if dealing with normals (82) (105). At the same time the child's attention span should be "stretched" so that he can perhaps learn to concentrate upon all educational experiences for progressively longer periods of time. To switch activities the moment the retarded child loses interest would be self-defeating. The teacher, rather, should attempt to offer the child another challenge using the same activity, or in other ways encourage him to spend increasing periods of time in the performance of motor tasks (30).

In general, it is held that frequent and short practice periods are better for the retardate than prolonged and oppressive ones (69). The retardate can rarely perceive the long range influences of participation in manual and gross motor activities upon his future development. He works and plays at motor activities because of the *here and now,* because he is *immediately* attracted by the task or by the other rewarding circumstances in the current situation. To expect a child with learning difficulties to work vigorously in exercise programs "because it is going to do him some good" would seem to be a somewhat optimistic outlook on the part of a physical education teacher.

The Additive Method. It is a time-worn assumption that when working with retarded children one must reduce the complexity to simplicities, one must teach by the "part method" rather than introducing the child to the complex whole. It is similarly true that many brain-injured children, or ones whose mental impairment may stem from environ-mental factors, find great difficulty synthesizing experience (27) (72) (98) (101).

These children often have a difficult time building the "whole" out of the parts. Thus the method perhaps best employed is to first teach a simple component of a task, one which the retarded child can master, and then to pair this component with a second, and then to practice these two in unison. A third component may then be added, as motor skills are invariably a series of acts, and then these three practiced as a unit. This should be continued until the entire complex task is performed as a whole.

The extent to which a skill or a skill component is considered a "whole" depends upon the complexity of the learner. Skipping can usually be mastered as a whole by a normal youngster as he copies a peer's actions. A child with perceptual-motor problems, however, must first be helped to posture on one foot while an educable retardate might first be aided to learn how to hop twice on one foot and then two times on the other, prior to learning to skip (30). In other terms the quickest and thus the more satisfying learning occurs when the child is introduced to as much of the whole as he is capable of organizing. To fragment a skill into components too small can be as deadly as presenting too complex a portion of the task to the child with learning problems (30).

Who Should Teach? One central problem in teaching methodology involves the nature of the teacher. Who should teach retardates? The physical educator, the special educator, therapist, or just who? What about the sex of the teacher as related to the sex of the child? Should women teach girls, and should boys be led by men?

The assumption of gender in normal children usually occurs somewhere between the fourth and sixth year as the child indicates his allegiance to one or the other sex by the assumption of patterns of speech, movement, and emotional makeup which the society usually associates with men and women (28) (114) (117). The retardate frequently has problems making this appropriate identification. It is frequent to see, for example, an excess of girl-like behaviors in groups of retarded boys. They smile too much, giggle inappropriately, and otherwise indicate that they have not begun to identify with the elder members of their own sex.

It is believed that for the above reasons, whenever possible, retarded boys should be confronted with masculine figures when led in physical activities. They should see appropriate male models of behavior so that they might imitate the gestures, motor skills, speech patterns, and all the subtle and obvious behaviors which are considered masculine in our society.

Similarly, girls who are retarded should be led and encouraged by women who are capable of presenting to them appropriate activities and models of feminine behavior. Dance activities should be included in programs for girls, not only to elicit the improvement which rhythmics have been demonstrated to induce in retarded children, but also because the graceful movements emanating from dance are considered appropriate and desirable signs of femininity, signs which it is important that retarded and neurologically handicapped girls evidence.

The training of physical educators who work with retarded should include at least one, and preferably more than one, course in special education, containing material which helps to orient them to general information regarding retardation, as well as to educational principles which govern the improvement of the neurologically handicapped. At the same time, special educators interested in education through the physical should participate in courses containing information regarding the nature of physical activity and motor development of normals, as well as developmental sequences of activities and games appropriate to programs for the re-tarded and neurologically handicapped.

It is believed that teachers with a background in physical activity as well as teachers whose primary interest is in the physical education can make a valuable contribution through motor activities. However, both groups of teachers should obtain content in courses within the college "major" of the other. Curriculum conferences have recently been held at the national level to formulate guidelines for the content of these inter-disciplinary courses.

Guided Discovery. Thirty years ago, certain physical educators, taking their cue from John Dewey submitted philosophical statements which encouraged the use of democratic approach when teaching physical activities. Only within recent years, however, has an author contrived a workable approach to leading a child through physical activities to the point where he may truly begin to think constructively about his own actions (84). Taking principles of cognition outlined by Bruner (20), Mosston has presented a framework worthy of consideration by all teachers, whether they be in physical education, special education, or general education (84).

Essentially Mosston holds that true education can occur only when the child is presented with alternatives and must deal with them. And to achieve this decision making and mediating behavior the physical educator must gradually relinquish to the student various decisions inherent in the teaching-learning environment.

Mosston's methodology is too global for a thorough review here; however, it is believed that many of his statements hold important promise for the physical educator dealing with retarded and neurologically handicapped youth. If in some ways retarded children seem animal-like, it is believed that enhancement of their human qualities will not come about as a physical educator commands them like a lion tamer. After they have proved that they can begin to exert self-control and to take responsibilities for at least some levels of their behavior, they should be given opportunities to do so. To lead exercises "by the numbers" in a loud voice in front of a group of retarded boys indicates little except that the teacher's strength of physique and/or personality exceeds that of his charges. The physical educator in a special school or institution should view himself as a partner in the general educational program, not just as the person best suited to elicit large muscles.

It thus is believed more constructive if the physical educator, while presenting a "tight" structure initially to a group of retardates, later may relinquish some of the decisions to them. Modifying directions from a "walk this balance beam at a time like this" to "let's see how many ways you can walk the beam" encourages children to think about their actions, to make decisions and to place themselves under their own control, all important goals for the youngster with learning problems (30) (33).

Later the children may be able to make an even greater variety of decisions, including the construction of an obstacle course containing a balance beam, or perhaps may evaluate each other in a team situation. Leading a child through the most observable kind of behavior he engages in, from situations wherein he merely responds to external commands to situations in which he begins to make decisions about his own actions, would seem to be the most constructive way in which physical education activities may be employed in the total educational program for children with learning difficulties.

SUMMARY

The retarded child is more inclined to feel and to move, rather than to think and act. The extent to which the physical educator can encourage the latter sequence, it would seem, is a gauge to his value in the total educational program for the retardate. It is contingent upon the physical educator to offer more than just the opportunity to grow large muscles to retarded and neurologically handicapped children.

Retarded and neurologically handicapped children, to be taught best, should:

1...Engage in tasks which offer an optimum of novelty and complexity; and these tasks must be frequently modified while remaining within a correct sequence of difficulty (82).

2...Be confronted by teachers who offer them appropriate masculine or feminine patterns of behavior to emulate (114).

3...Be led to *think* about what they are doing, and through graded experiences be offered more and more decisions within the teacher-learning environment (84).

4...Be offered as much of the whole of a task as they seem capable of grasping (101).

5...Be taught by teachers with sufficient backgrounds both in special education and in physical education so they know some of the *whys* behind the techniques they are employing, teachers who can discuss intelligently the theoretical frameworks which attempt to link thinking, physical activity, perception and verbal behavior.

6...Engage in spaced rather than massed practice, particularly if the task is boring or physically taxing.

7...Be taught specifically the relationships between skills or sub-skills in which it is hoped transfer of training will occur (39).

8...Be given knowledge that he is responsible for the retention of a skill, prior to the skill being learned (75).

9...Be required to overlearn a skill which it is hoped he will retain (27).

10...Be rewarded by praise when appropriate, and given this reinforcement for even slight improvement in abilities.

11...Be placed in situations in which social punishment from their peers will not retard motor performance and learning.

CHAPTER IV
PERCEPTIONS OF THE BODY AND OF ITS POSITIONS IN SPACE

During the first weeks of life, the normal infant begins to gain an awareness of his body parts and of his position in space (11) (49) (60) (90). It is not unusual to notice an infant only a few days old fixing his gaze for prolonged periods of time upon his hand (49). Later he begins gaining an awareness of his body surfaces as he turns in his crib. By the age of six the normal child is usually able to identify his left and right hands (49) (88), and by the age of eight or nine can move into the reference of another person and determine correctly whether the one they are watching is moving to their left or right (49).

The body image of the normal adolescent and adult continues to change as they mature (37) (68). The abrupt changes during adolescence, if not perceived as desirable, are the signs for direct efforts on the part of youths to change their shapes (68). The male may attempt to build his body with exercise while the girl may either pad the concavities or attempt to diet away desirable convexities.

It is a ubiquitious finding that retardates form no such stable image of themselves (30). Rarely can a mongoloid child or a retardate with an I.Q. of less than sixty correctly identify his left or right hand. Similarly children with perceptual-motor problems are often unable to correctly locate their body relative to objects, nor can they correctly determine where objects are relative to them (30) (68) (121).

The importance of these basic perceptions to the movements of children has been attested to frequently in literature based upon clinical evidence. It has been asserted that faulty perceptions regarding the body will necessarily impair movement. Conversely others have suggested that inability to move well will inhibit the perceptual judgments relative to the body, its parts and their relation to objects in space (71).

Recently the writer obtained an extremely high correlation between measures of body image and the combined performance score in a variety of motor activities including those involving balance, agility, and ball throwing and catching (30). Although this kind of relationship does not necessarily infer causality, *i.e.* it is unclear whether poor motor ability contributes to faulty body perception or the reverse is true, it is believed that specific training in some of the attributes outlined in the pages which follow will contribute to the perceptually organizing base (their body) from which the retardate and the neurologically handicapped youngster may make more complex perceptual judgments.

Instruments purporting to evaluate the "body-image" or perception of the body have taken many diverse forms (2) (12). Some depend upon the extent to which the child or adult "projects himself" into pictures, ink blots, or similar measures. The draw-a-person task, for example, is purportedly a measure of body image (2).

Several in use depend upon the accuracy with which a child can touch his body parts, and those of a man in a picture, when asked to do so. A recently developed tool assesses body image by noting the accuracy with which a child can imitate the gestures of the experimenter (15). These latter instruments have been criticized on the basis that they are heavily dependent upon the child's vocabulary or upon his ability to copy a demonstration.

Clinicians have not been remiss in suggesting various methods for heightening the child's perceptions of himself. Trampoline jumping, for example, is frequently prescribed to give the child an acute awareness of his body's surfaces as he lands on them (35) (71). Other techniques have included lying on a mat and moving the limbs while pressing them against the floor (71).

Evaluation of children who have been exposed to various training techniques usually reveal subtle or obvious developmental gaps. For example, it has been a frequent finding of the author that while many children can correctly identify their left arms and legs when asked to do so, fewer can react accurately when asked to lie on their left sides or place their right sides nearest an object.

Thus it is believed that a sound developmental series involving the perception of the body should also assess the child's ability to assume various positions relative to objects. As an outcome of a recent investigation the author has developed the sixteen-step sequence, which is outlined on the following pages. While research is presently being undertaken to further validate the order of these steps, it is believed it provides a comprehensive assessment tool which might be applied to all retarded and neurologically handicapped children. The findings of such an assessment should suggest training methods which will provide a helpful accompaniment to any program of motor education.

This sequence is based upon the following assumptions. (1) Perception of the body is continuous with the body's relationship to objects in space (49) (71). (2) Awareness of the body surfaces—front, back, side, etc.—is more basic than the ability to make various left-right discriminations (3) (30). A comprehensive program of body awareness should involve a variety of activities, with the child constantly interacting, at whatever level he can, by demonstrating various relationships between his body and objects in space.

These sixteen steps may be divided into five subcategories. (1) The perception of body planes and their relationship to objects in space (steps #1-3); (2) the perception of body parts and the movement of these parts (steps #4-5); (3) the awareness of the left-right dimensions of the body, the possible unilateral movements the body may make, and the location of objects relative to its left-right dimensions (steps #6-10); (4) using a personal reference system, the determination of the left-right dimensions of objects (step #11); (5) moving into the personal reference of another individual and determining the left and right hands, legs, etc., and the unilateral movements of another person (steps #11-16).

Following each step in this sequence are suggested testing activities purporting to evaluate the acquisition of the step involved. It is suggested that the teacher or parent should begin at step one and move down the check list attempting to determine when a child evidences the inability to accomplish the sub-tasks correctly. After this occurs for two to three steps, the check list should be temporarily abandoned and various tasks should be administered which are intended to improve the deficiencies identified. Many of these activities may be combined with various other motor training procedures suggested in the chapters which follow. For example, when attempting to heighten concepts of laterality the child may be encouraged to verbalize when he is rolling to the left or to the right on a mat. Thus, agility and laterality are being trained simultaneously. Similarly various tasks purporting to heighten balance can be combined with laterality training.

SIXTEEN DEVELOPMENTAL STEPS IN THE FORMATION OF THE BODY IMAGE AND THE BODY'S POSITION IN SPACE

1. IDENTIFICATION OF BODY PLACES (FRONT, BACK, SIDES, TOP, BOTTOM).
   a. Touch the front of your body.....................
   b. Touch the top of your head ....
   c. Touch your side...............................
2. BODY PLANES IN RELATION TO OBJECTS.
   a. Touch the wall with your back...................
   b. Lie on the mat on your side ....
   c. Place your front toward the chair................
3. OBJECTS IN RELATION TO BODY PLANES.
   a. Where is the ball—in front of you, behind you, or by your side?...................
   b. Is the ball by your feet or by your head?...........
   c. Is the chair to your side, to your back, or to your front? ....
4. BODY PART IDENTIFICATION (LIMBS, ETC.).
   a. Where are your feet? touch your feet...............
   b. Where is your arm?........ touch your shoulder ....
   c. Where is your leg?...... touch your elbow ....
5. MOVEMENTS OF THE BODY.
   A. TRUNK MOVEMENT WHILE FIXED
      a. Bend forward toward the front ....
      b. Bend to the side; bend to the other side ....
      c. Bend slowly backwards ....
   B. GROSS MOVEMENTS IN RELATION TO BODY PLANES.
      a. Where is your side?.... Can you move sideways?....
      b. Let's try forward..... backward..... and sideways movements..........
      c. How can you jump up?..............

C. LIMB MOVEMENTS.
    a. What can you do with your arms? Straighten arms
    .... bend arms...... lift arms at your shoulder
    ..... turn your arms (rotate them both ways).....
    b. What can you do with your legs? Straighten legs
    ...... bend one leg at your knee......
    c. Lift one leg at your hip......

6. LATERALITY OF BODY.
    a. Touch your left leg...........
    b. Touch your right arm............
    c. Climb this ladder using your left leg and left arm first
    ....
    d. Touch your right ear............

7. LATERALITY IN RELATION TO OBJECTS.
    a. Place your left side nearest the chair ....
    b. Put your left foot on the box..........
    c. Go up to the wall and put your right side nearest the
    wall, now move and touch the wall with your left side
    ....

8. STATIC OBJECTS RELATED TO LATERALITY.
    a. Is that box by your right side?...............
    b. Is that stick touching your right or left foot? ....
    c. Which arm is nearest the ball?.........

9. LATERALITY AND MOVING OBJECTS.
    a. You stand still and I'll move around you. You tell me
    where I am. When am I nearest your back, nearest your
    left, and nearest your right?.........
    b. Now I'll move a little faster. You tell me where I am
    now.........
    c. Stand still and tell me where the rolling ball is ....
    Is it to your left, your right, your back, or your front?
    ....

10. MOVING BODY'S LATERALITY IN RELATION TO OBJECTS.
    a. You walk around this chair and tell me where the
    chair is in relation to you ....
    b. Using two chairs around which to walk a figure-eight,
    walk around the chairs and tell me where you are.
    When are your left and right sides of your body near
    the nearest chair?...............

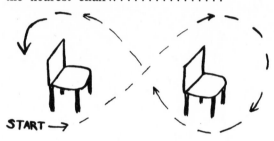

11. THE LEFT AND RIGHT OF OBJECTS (PERSONAL REFERENCE SYSTEM).
    a. Point to the left side of the table.................
    b. Point to the right side of the chair ....
    c. Show me the right and left sides of the paper ....

In steps 12-16 the child is not moving, but is asked to make judgments of another's body parts or movements.

12. STATIC DIRECTIONALITY WITH OTHER PEOPLE (PROTECTION INTO ANOTHER'S REFERENCE SYSTEM).
    a. (Person opposite child) Show me my left arm . . . .
    b. Touch my right elbow . . . .
    c. Touch my left ear with your left hand. . . . .

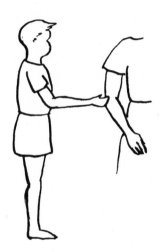

13. LATERALITY OF OTHER PEOPLE IN RELATION TO STATIC OBJECTS.
    a. Which side of my body is nearest the chair? . . . .
    b. As I walk around the figure eight (the two chairs) tell me which side of the object is nearest to me? . . . .

14. RELATION OF STATIC OBJECTS TO LATERALITY OF OTHER PEOPLE.
    a. (Teacher moves chair to a static position) Where is this chair in relation to me? . . . .
    Is it at my left or at my right? . . . .
    b. Where is the ladder in relation to me? . . . .

15. MOVING OBJECTS IN RELATION TO OTHERS' LATERALITY.
    a. Tell me where the ball is as it moves around my body. Is it to my right, my left, my front, or my back? . . . .
    b. Where is the moving rope? Is it to my front, my back, my left, or my right? . . . .

16. LATERALITY OF OTHERS' MOVEMENTS.
    a. Tell me, am I walking to my left or my right? . . . .
    b. Which way am I moving? . . . .

TRAINING PROCEDURES

Body image training *must* involve transfer (5) (23). The practice of a few favorite exercises to heighten laterality, for example, has been shown to train *only* those exercises and at times will fail to give the child a generalized concept that two sides of his body are independent of each other, that they can function independently or in unison, and that one is called "left," and the other is named "right." Thus a variety of tasks should be employed to aid the child to form the desirable perceptions. Some of these are obviously dictated by the level on the check list reached by the child. Others may be devised by the teacher. These activities fall into several categories.

(1) **Contact of body surfaces and body parts to various surfaces of the environment.** The child may be asked to roll to his back on the mat, later to his side, and last to his front. He may be asked to move against a wall and to place his back, side, or front toward the wall while maintaining

contact. Limb movements may be made while contacting the vertical surfaces of walls, or the horizontal surfaces of matted floors. These movements may be paired with verbal cues from the teacher, or by verbalization on the part of the retarded. Several of the initial steps within the developmental sequence may be accomplished with this kind of approach, primarily numbers 1, 2, 3, 4, 5, and 6.

(2) **Pairing words with movements.** The extent to which the child can move or otherwise make correct judgments when asked to do so verbally has been assessed on the check list. This approach can be utilized in various training tasks after the child's perceptual limits have been ascertained. "Simon Says" games can be used here.

(3) **Drawing and Visual Inspection.** While lying or standing against a wall containing a writing surface the teacher or another child can outline the body, or some of its parts with a marking pen. The child can step away and study his body's conformations; perhaps color them, and in other ways discuss and think about what he has drawn and what it represents.

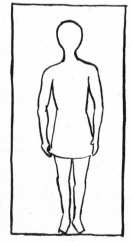

(4) **Unilateral movements.** Movements to the left or right can be made in a variety of ways in response to word cues by the teacher, accompanied by word cues on the part of the child, or in response to word cues given by the child prior to his movements. An example of these activities include: rolling or tumbling movements to the left or right; jumping and turning to the left and right; crawling on the hands and knees; and calling out "left and right" as the hands touch the mat; jumping or moving laterality to the left or right; climbing and naming the hand used on each rung of a ladder; and kicking and/or throwing movements with accompanying verbalizations.

(5) **Activities while one hand is occupied.** A ball may be held in one identified hand while walking the balance beam. Similarly a brightly colored cuff may be placed on one wrist. A variety of visual cues may be elicited to improve the child's awareness of his left-right dimensions.

SUMMARY

It is believed by many that the child's body forms the "platform" from which he makes perceptual judgments about space (49) (71). For example, it is easy to see that successful completion of step number 11 leads naturally to various left-right discriminations necessary to begin reading. Words must be read in correct order from left to right, letters must be placed in words in correct left-right order, and more basically many letters and numbers have individual left-right dimensions which must be perceived before the child can be expected to spell or to read.

It is believed that the perceptions which are covered in this chapter are basic to all kinds of learnings on the part of the retarded child. For if the child is unaware of where he is, what he is doing with himself, and where his body parts are, how can he be expected to engage in more exact judgments inherent in most classroom tasks?

foot, and determine if he can maintain the position for more than six seconds. (the foot should be fixed)

CHAPTER V
BALANCE

Balance involves the ability of an individual to maintain equilibrium relative to gravity, and is usually evaluated with various kinds of visual and/or motor stresses imposed. A recent investigation by the author indicated that balance tasks provided the scores most predictive of performance of a number of perceptual-motor activities when a subject population of educable retardates and neurologically handicapped children were evaluated (30).

Balance ability should probably be considered in the plural in the case of normal mature individuals. Factorial studies have found that, in this kind of subject population, four independent attributes involving balance may be identified (45): (a) Static balance, *i.e.,* posturing on one foot or across a narrow edge with vision; (b) Dynamic balance, movement in relatively large amount of space while attempting to maintain an upright posture, *i.e.,* walking a balance beam; (c) Balance without vision, maintaining equilibrium with eyes closed; and (d) Balancing objects. While these factors are probably not as independent in the case of children with motor problems, it is indicative of the breadth of balance activities which should be utilized when attempting to improve this important attribute (30) (34).

The Evaluation of Balance. To evaluate a child's balance the teacher or parent may simply ask him to stand on one

If he can accomplish this initial task he may then be asked to maintain a one-foot stand while keeping his arms folded across his chest.

If this can be done for more than four seconds, further difficulty can be presented by requesting that he balance, arms unfolded, on one foot with his eyes closed.

If the child can accomplish this latter task it is probable that extensive work in balance training is not necessary. On the other hand, if he fails to maintain an eyes-closed balance it is usually indicative of some basic neuro-motor problem which should be given the attention it deserves.

Generally speaking mongoloid children without special training cannot be expected to balance on one foot for more than two seconds. Trainable retardates can usually balance for about four seconds. Neurologically handicapped children balance considerably better and, on the average, can posture on one foot for about four seconds without vision. Educable retardates can usually hold this position without vision slightly longer (30).

Balance will not improve without specific training particularly in the case of children with severe problems, *i.e.* the mongoloid. Balance underlies a number of more complex motor attributes, including various kinds of agility tasks, throwing, running, skipping, catching balls, etc. It is a basic factor which deserves an important part in any program designed to improve the ability of children with mild neurological impairments, and/or mental deficiencies (9) (71).

Sequential Activities to Improve Balance. Four sequences are presented on the pages which follow. Generally a child should participate in at least two of these, one a sequence of static tasks, the other a dynamic sequence, working on tasks at the level determined by his observed capacities. Two of these sequences involve static balance, the other two moving balance problems. The order of these tasks has been arrived at by an examination of experimental evidence

(45), as well as by attempting to "fill in" various gaps in our knowledge about balance by subjective speculation. As further data becomes available one should refine and adjust the order of tasks accordingly.

These series consist of tasks involving static balance with the body's center of mass near the floor. Static balance tasks while standing, dynamic balance tasks in which varying degrees of task difficulty are imposed, and dynamic balance tasks in which varying degrees of visual stress are involved are all important.

The following sequences are to be taken as suggested activities, rather than as the *only* helpful balance tasks in which a child might engage. The child should be encouraged to explore other possibilities, as they become able to work within the structure initially imposed by the teacher.

PHASE I, STATIC BALANCE ON A MAT

The more basic activities in this category can be explored with benefit by children classified as evidencing Down's Syndrome and by children with mild to moderate cerebral palsy. The more complex tasks can be practiced with benefit by nearly all children with mild movement problems.

1. Seated balance; the attempt should be made to remain relatively immobile for increasingly lengthy periods of time.

2. Balancing while lying on the side.

(The child can also be encouraged to verbally identify the side upon which he is lying. Attempt to have the child place his entire side nearest the mat.)

3. Hand and knee balance, four points touching the mat.

4. Hand and knee balance on three points, lifting either one hand or foot from the mat.

6. Hand and knee balance, two points (cross pattern) *i.e.* left arm and right leg in the air.

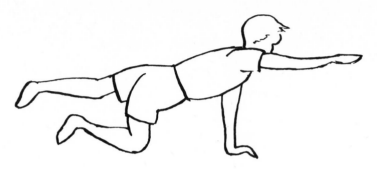

5. Upright kneeling.

7. Hand and knee balance, two points, same side.

8. Hand and knee balance, with modifications, two and three points. The child might be asked to posture on three points one of which is an elbow; or perhaps to use a three-point balance with his back nearest the mat.

9. Same knee-foot balance, two points.

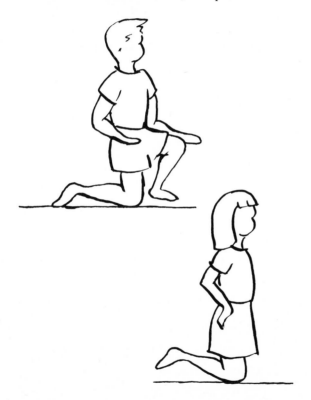

10. Knee only balance, two points.

PHASE II, STATIC BALANCE, WHILE STANDING

Most children, who have proceeded to step seven in the initial sequence above may begin to posture on one foot while standing (step 4 in this sequence). Additionally most children with more severe balance problems can begin to work on balances in this category which involve posturing on both feet (steps one through three).

1. Standing on a line, feet parallel.

2. Feet and heels together.

3. Heel-to-toe standing, feet on an imaginary line.

9. Combinations, eyes closed, knee-high, arms folded.

4. One-foot balance.
5. One foot, knee-high.
6. One foot, arms folded.
7. One foot, eyes closed.
8. One foot, eyes closed, arms folded.

Care should be taken not to make the tasks an endurance test, by asking that the child spend prolonged periods of time in their performance. Additionally, time should be taken to encourage balance on the non-preferred foot in all of these tasks.

PHASE III, DYNAMIC BALANCE WITH TASK MODIFICATIONS

It is obvious that with balance beams of decreasing width, dynamic balance on their surfaces becomes more difficult. Additionally, task difficulty can be increased by requiring that the child perform various movements, *i.e.* walking over obstacles while walking down the beam. This sequence, therefore, assumes that the walking is being carried out on a beam 20' long whose width permits the child to traverse its length without falling off. The author has found that beams whose surfaces are slanted or whose widths decrease in a regular fashion are excellent instruments for increasing balance proficiency.

1. Walking forward.
2. Moving sideways.

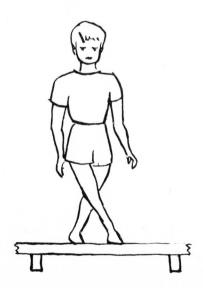

3. Walking forward over obstacles, on the beam.

4. Walking forward under obstacles on the beam, one foot shorter than the performer.

5. Walking forward over obstacles, one foot over the beam.

7. Walking backwards on the beam.

8. Walking backwards over obstacles on the beam.

9. Walking backwards, obstacles one foot high over the beam.

6. Walking sideways over obstacles, place one foot over the beam.

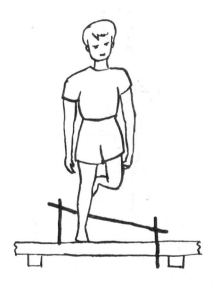

PHASE IV. DYNAMIC BALANCE WITH VISUAL STRESS

Balance is closely aligned with vision (30) (119). Deprivation of visual cues invariably causes more difficulty with more balance tasks in most children.[3] There are varying degrees of visual control which can be exerted over dynamic balance tasks by the performer. The sequence which follows requires that the child exert less and less visual attention to the task, thus requiring that he develop a kinesthetic awareness of foot placement, body position, etc., without the usual aid of direct visual inspection. It is again assumed that the balance beam is on a minimal width 4" which permits the child to traverse its surface without leaving it; and that it is about 20' long.

It is possible, of course, to integrate various phase tasks presented in the previous sections with the tasks outlined in this one.

1. Forward walking, eyes looking at the beam and feet as they move.

---

[3]The author has, on occasion, found that a child with severe perceptual problems relative to the organization of visual space will balance better with his eyes closed than when they are open!

2. Forward walking, eyes on a point moved slightly ahead of the performer by the teacher at a speed determined by the performer.

3. Forward walking, eyes on a fixed point to the front at the end of the beam, and then at eye level.

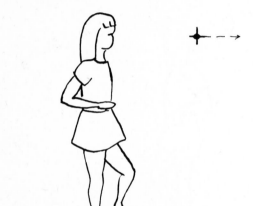

4. Forward walking, eyes on a point moving up and down, at the end of the beam.

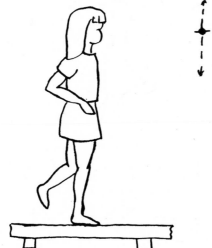

5. Walking forward with eyes on a point moving from left to right.

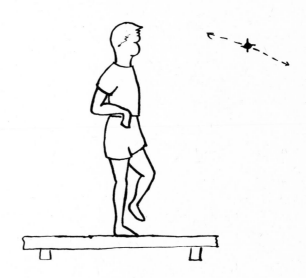

6. Forward walking with watching rotating objects to the front.

This sequence can be repeated with added difficulty by placing the visual targets to the side of the beam.

Overview. Balance involves an integration of the body's balance mechanisms in the inner ear, reflexive control by the large anti-gravity muscles, as well as conscious integration by the cortex (20). Balance training in various positions other than standing has been shown to transfer positively to standing balance. Balance training may be either in static relatively immobile positions, or in dynamic moving tasks. Both types of tasks should be incorporated into a child's training program.

Balance tasks are made progressively more difficult by imposing variations in the manner in which the eyes may be used, by varying the difficulty of the walking surface (narrowing the beam, or tilting it), by imposing obstacles to negotiate while walking a beam, by requiring that the performer change his center of gravity as he performs, and/or by requiring that the individual depend upon fewer bodily supports as he attempts to maintain his equilibrium.

Balance training is particularly important to the child with mild to moderate perceptual-motor problems, to the mongoloid child, and to the child diagnosed as evidencing mild or moderate cerebral palsey. Balance underlies more complex agility tasks, throwing, catching and similar activities which in turn underlie the performance of most sports skills and of certain classroom activities.

CHAPTER VI
LOCOMOTION

Locomotion is an interesting and complex facet of man's behavior. Walking is contributed to by a number of basic reflexes, which are triggered by pressure to the bottom of the feet, and by the reciprocal actions of the arms and legs (90). Walking is also controlled partially by the higher brain centers as well as being timed and modified by the cerebellum, reticular activating systems, and other neural structures.

Training in basic locomotion and in variations of locomotor activities forms an important part of most programs of motor education (30) (71). Emphasis should be placed on the locomotor activities it is found the child cannot perform, rather than simply practicing activities which have been obviously mastered by the child (95).

In infancy several basic reflexes are present which later seem to blend into the infant's efforts at normal locomotion (90). Some of these include a reflex pattern which involves walking itself! Infants a few hours old, if pressure is applied to the bottoms of their feet and their trunks are supported, will move their legs in a normal walking pattern. Various righting reflexes are seen at birth which also contribute to the development of normal walking. If a newborn child is held head down, or head back, he will flex his trunk muscles as he attempts to regain an upright position (90) (94).

In many children with mild to moderate coordination problems, however, this subtle blend of involuntary and voluntary movements does not result in an efficient and appropriate gait pattern (7). Abnormal flexions are seen in the arms and at times unusual extensions are seen in the legs as the child attempts to walk. Similarly, the arms and legs may not be coordinated correctly when walking and crawling. For example, as the child walks, the left arm may not move forward with the right leg. Similarly, the right knee and right hand may not touch the floor at the same time when the child attempts to crawl (35).

Some programs of motor education place virtually their entire emphasis upon locomotor activities (35). It is not believed, however, productive to force a child to crawl who is already evidencing a proficient crawling pattern. There is no research evidence to indicate that practice in locomotor activities does anything but improve the task practiced (95).

At the same time locomotor activities are important. Particularly when they are paired with various kinds of problems involving visual-motor coordination. Children with moderate perceptual-motor problems have been consistently found to have difficulties coordinating movements simultaneously on both sides of their bodies (7) (30). Crawling and walking in a correct manner obviously involve such intergration.

The Evaluation of Locomotor Proficiency. To evaluate a child's basic locomotor capacities, at least five tasks should be required of him: crawling, walking, hopping forward on one foot, jumping forward using both feet simultaneously and jumping backwards using both feet. While it may also be helpful to ask the child to skip and/or to gallop, these latter activities are often "sex-linked," *i.e.*, boys gallop while girls skip.

If a child evidences an appropriate cross-extension

pattern in his crawling and walking efforts, can hop at least three times on one foot, and can jump forwards and backwards at least three times, he should then be asked to attempt the three latter activities with more accuracy, *i.e.,* ask him to jump into four to six squares 1' by 1'. If the child can accomplish these latter tasks, relatively little time should be spent upon basic locomotor activities, and he can then proceed to more complex activities involving change of direction, ball handling and other game skills.

It is usual to find that only about 10% of retarded children, not otherwise impaired motorically, cannot crawl or walk with appropriate cross-extension pattern. Even a mongoloid child, while unable to balance well, thus walks with his legs spread wide; nonetheless, he usually moves his arms and legs appropriately when crawling and walking (30).

However, from one-third to one-half of the children evidencing mild to moderate perceptual-motor problems may not crawl and walk well (30).

A large percentage of children with general learning problems have problems jumping and hopping with any degree of accuracy. Only about one-third can be expected to jump into one-foot squares with any accuracy, while only about 15% can be expected to hop or to jump backwards with accuracy into similar patterns (30). Thus, tasks of the latter kind, locomotion with the necessity for accuracy and control, are more to be emphasized in motor education programs, as opposed to merely crawling, jumping, etc., without the necessity to do so accurately.

In general, movement backwards is difficult for children with coordination problems (30). It is not unusual to find that a child can hop forward on one foot with more accuracy and control than he can jump backwards from two feet (30).

Often children who may have problems moving one side of their body, due to some neurological impairment in the motor areas in the opposite cerebral hemisphere may be able to hop forward on their "good" leg better than they can jump forward using two feet, one of which does not function well.

It is important, therefore, when evaluating a child's locomotor abilities to attempt to ascertain how well he moves in the usual locomotor activities, *i.e.,* walking, crawling, etc., but also how well he can hop and jump with accuracy, and at the same time how well he can move backwards.

Developmental Sequences for the Training of Locomotor Balance. Balance ability underlies many of the more complex locomotor activities. If balance is severely impaired, the child will only fail when confronted with various locomotor tasks that are more complex. For example, unless a child can posture for several seconds on one foot, he cannot be expected to hop and to land on that foot. And, of course, if the child cannot hop accurately on one foot he cannot be expected to skip rhythmically, which is essentially a hop-shuffle movement, alternating feet.

The sequences illustrated in the pages which follow are of two types. The initial one is a sequence of activities in which relatively unstructured locomotor activities are pictured; the second in which the child must exercise more control over his movements.

PHASE I. LOCOMOTOR ABILITY

1. Crawling with handprints.

2. Knee crawling—vigorous shoulder action.

4. Jumping in place, with arm swing.

3. Walking with foot-prints.

5. Jumping forward in succession with arm swing.
6. One foot hopping in place.
7. Hopping in rhythm, alternating feet: two times on one foot and then two times on the other, three and three, or more difficult combinations *i.e.* two on one foot and three hops on the other.
8. Jumping backwards, with a controlled landing.
9. Galloping.
10. Skipping.

PHASE II. ADVANCED LOCOMOTOR ACTIVITIES

2. Jump forward in succession over several lines.

1. Jump forward, backward, and sideways over a line.

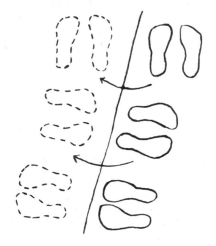

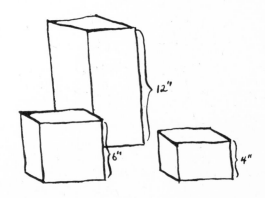

3. Jump from varying heights, with proper landing.

4. Hop forward over a line, backwards, and sideways.

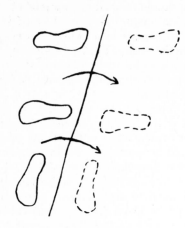

6. Jump backwards over a line, and then over a succession of lines.

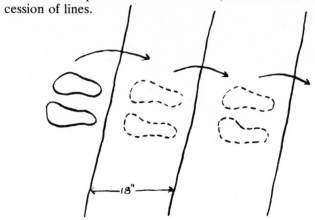

5. Hop forward over a succession of lines.

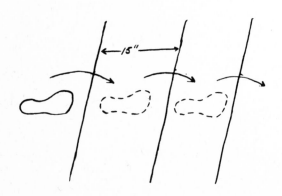

7. Jump forward and sideways over a height.

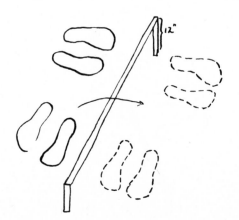

8. Hop over a height.

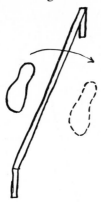

9. Jump backward over a height.

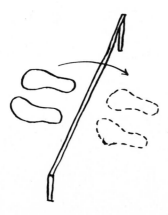

SUMMARY

Children should then be encouraged to modify loco-motor activities, and conditions should be presented which encourage them to engage in a complex program of loco-motor activities in the form of lines, or consisting of obstacles to negotiate. When possible these locomotor activities should be incorporated into rhythmical activities. Performing them to music is also motivating.

Certain important points should be remembered when attempting to improve locomotion. A cross-extension pattern should be evidenced at all times; the arm movement on one side should be similar to the leg movement on the opposite side. When jumping the arms should lift and extend at the same time the legs extend. When landing the child should be encouraged to ascend from risers of increasing height, and should be given specific instructions involving the quick knee bend executed to take the shock of landing.

CHAPTER VII
AGILITY

Agility may be defined as the ability to quickly and accurately move the body through a reasonably complex movement or a series of movements. Underlying agility is balance, accurate locomotion, power, and the ability to integrate various of the body parts into a coordinated act (45).

Agility training reflects a combination of attributes, and is important prior to the child learning more complex sports skills (34) (45). For unless a child can move his body quickly and accurately in the pathway of a moving ball, he cannot hope to catch it. His ability to move backwards and laterally are likewise requisite to participating in most games valued by his peers.

Several kinds of agility tasks may be considered, and are outlined on the pages which follow. (a) Locomotor agility in which the individual is combining various locomotor activities (74) into complex acts involving rapid changes of directions, and (b) agility movements in which the body does not change its location in space as drastically as when the child participates in a dodge run.

The concept of agility is too global for a thorough review here (94). The variety of tasks which reflect this attribute may be only suggested in the pages which follow. Agility is a reflection of the manner in which the child can direct the "orchestra of muscles" with which he is endowed, the extent to which he can move quickly with accuracy and with purpose.

The Evaluation of Agility. One method of evaluating agility is to ask the child to lie on his back, his feet toward the teacher. He may then be asked to get up "as rapidly as you can," and complete the movement "facing me" (*i.e.,* the teacher). If he can arise in about one second it is indicative of a generally agile child. On the other hand, if a child over the age of six takes longer than two seconds to accomplish this, or must first roll to his stomach, "clamber" to his hands and knees, arise, and then turn and face the teacher again, it is indicative of a moderate agility problem[1] (30).

The average mongoloid child will have to first turn to his stomach, and then arise, and usually will take between two and four seconds to complete the task. Trainable and educable retardates will usually remain facing the teacher, but will take about three seconds to complete the movement; children classified as neurologically handicapped will also require about three seconds to get up while a child not evidencing motoric impairment can complete the action in about one-third the time (30).

General locomotor agility can be determined by reference to the child's ability to move backwards, to hop, and to jump with accuracy (See Chapter VI, page 38). The sequences of agility activities provided on the pages which follow include both activities involving locomotor agility, as well as those involving integration of the body parts, without accompanying locomotor activity.

---

[1]Difficulty in this kind of task may stem from weak abdominals, inability to coordinate arm push on the floor, trunk flexion, leg action, or from a combination of stretch-coordination problems. Only a more thorough evaluation of the child can determine which of these reasons contributes to the inability to perform this task well.

3. Sequence: Back to the mat squat slowly, sit back placing one hand at a time on the mat, roll back to back-lying position, turn to stomach, move to hands and knees position, to the knees only and to a stand, one leg at a time.

PART I.
CONTROLLED ASCENDING AND DESCENDING

1. Sequence: Kneel one knee at a time and then move to a hand-knee position one hand moving to the mat at a time. Then move back to the knees only removing one hand at a time from the mat; and then finish the sequence standing, arising one foot at a time to a standing position again.

This must usually be demonstrated and performed before the child attempts it. The sequence may be simplified by including only four counts, *i.e.,* to both knees and then to a stand again. Movement may be speeded up to provide more difficulty.

2. Sequence: Kneel one knee at a time, then to a hand-knee position putting one hand at a time to the mat, and then descending further to the stomach by moving the legs backwards and the arms forward. The child should then roll over to his back, and then arise using the hands for assistance, to a standing position again.

4. Sequence: Side toward mat kneel on nearest knee, place same hand on mat, slowly slide to a side-lying position, roll to the back, to the other side, and then rise by pushing with the arm nearest the mat, moving to the knee, and then to a stand.

1. Sequence: Front Falling: From a standing position with the front of the body nearest the mat, relax knees, fall forward touching both knees at the same time, then the hands together. Regain the feet as rapidly as possible. Note, when falling forward, have the child lean slightly backwards.

2. Sequence: Side Falling: With the side nearest the mat, relax and fall sideways letting the knee nearest the mat touch first, placing the arm nearest the mat extended to the side, roll to the other side, and ascend quickly.

3. Sequence: Backwards Falling: Leaning forward, bend the knees and sit backwards to the mat, touching the hips before the hands reach back, roll to the back, knees high, and then roll over to the front-lying position, and regain the feet.

4. Sequence: Combinations of the above movements: With the back nearest the mat, turn and fall forwards, with the side nearest the mat turn and fall on the other side, with the front nearest the mat, turn and fall backwards. This combination may be accompanied by laterality training, *i.e.,* "with your back toward the mat, turn and fall on your left side."

Variety and control can be elicited from the activities within this sequence by asking the child to descend and/ or arise "as slowly as you can"... or request the child to perform some of these movements with his eyes closed.

PART III
MOVING AGILITY TASKS WITH
THE BODY NEAR THE MAT

1. "Log rolling, with combinations" rolling, attempting to maintain position on the mat, rolling with arms against sides, over head, etc.

2. Snake movement: Stomach in contact with the mat, pulling with arms, and using knees appropriately.

3. Knee and hand movements, forwards, backwards, laterally.

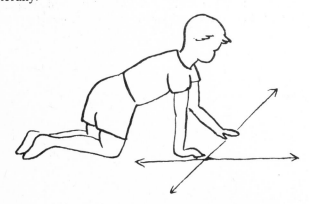

4. Hand-knee rolls, from a hand and knee position, roll sideways and regain the position. This sequence may be combined with laterality training, *i.e.*, "roll over your left shoulder to your left side."

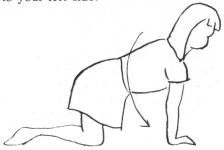

5. Ball rolls: Holding a "tuck" position, see how many directions you can roll.

6. Front somersaults using hands down a decline.

7. Back shoulder rolls down a decline, "crooked" back somersaults (should be preceded by Sequence #3 in Part II, which is found in this chapter). Place head to side opposite to that of shoulder rolled upon.

8. Back and front rolls on a level surface.

9. A series of the movements in parts 1-9 above, from two to three more.

The activities in this section should be preceded by the locomotor sequences contained in the previous chapter.

1. Sequence: Jump one-quarter and one-half turns in place, using the arms to lift and to turn the body.

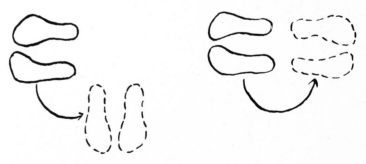

2. Sequence: Full jump turns from a two-foot stand to a two-foot landing.

3. Sequence: One foot balance to one-quarter and one-half turns landing on two feet.

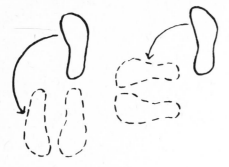

4. Sequence: One foot stand to one-quarter turns landing on one foot.

5. Sequence: Lateral movement, step-close-step, with increasing speed.

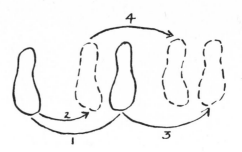

6. Sequence: Lateral movement, cross-stepping movement with increasing speed.

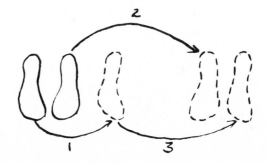

7. Sequence: Forward and backward running at various speeds with control stops, emphasize quick lowering of hips as the child attempts to stop.

Emphasis in these activities should be placed upon control, upon landing properly, and upon correct arm lift when jumping movements are involved. Most of these activities can be incorporated into games of low organization.

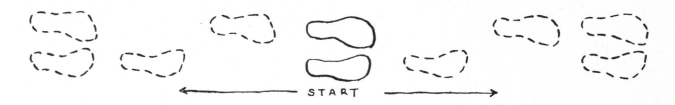

8. Sequence: Running backwards and laterally, and forward and laterally with control stops.

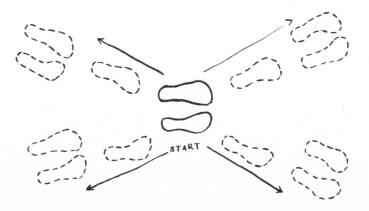

These sequences should not be carried to the point of fatigue, as fatigue can contribute to accidents. Many of the tasks, particularly those in these initial two sequences presented, may be carried out on a trampoline.

The running movements should be practiced until the child may not only initiate them well, but can also stop quickly and efficiently.

Agility training should involve participation in at least two of these sequences, one concerned with gross agility, *i.e.,* sequences one and two, and the second with locomotor agility (sequence #3). Agility work is intermediate between the more basic training in body-perception, balance, and locomotor activities, and the more advanced sports skills. It is believed that if a child has severe to moderate movement problems these more basic activities should be engaged in prior to attempting some of the more difficult tasks presented in this chapter.

CHAPTER VIII
STRENGTH, ENDURANCE, PLUS
FLEXIBILITY EQUALS FITNESS

Although the focus of the text is upon the development of a wide range of attributes, some of these basic abilities involve force (strength), sustaining an activity for a period of time (endurance), and moving through a range of motion (flexibility) (46) (64) (116). It is a well-documented fact that strength, endurance, and flexibility will only improve if the muscular and respiratory systems are overloaded in certain ways (6) (116). This overload must consist of an excess of resistance, or of repetitions, or of range of motion which the individual imposes upon himself, or is imposed upon him, to which he has not previously accommodated (46) (64) (116).

Thus simply engaging in exercises will not be as effective in producing change, as exercising to one's maximum. Merely moving the arms through a range of motion will not increase flexibility unless there is some attempt to increase that range of motion by persistent effort.

The reasons why an individual will overload his neuromuscular system are varied and many (110). However, the most effective method of encouraging effort, it is believed, is to develop a wide range of capacities, including balance, agility, as well as strength-endurance, so that the child will be successful at performing, and seek performance situations, perform to his maximum, and thus increase his capacities further. A trainable retardate will often not "put out" maximum effort when presented with exercises as he lacks the insight to perceive the long-term benefits of his efforts. The neurologically handicapped child must be encouraged to participate to his maximum either in simple exercises, or in more complex skills, before real improvement may be expected. Exercise capacities should be charted so that the child, if he is capable of understanding, may observe his gradual improvement.

Recent investigations of the strength and endurance of retarded and neurologically handicapped youth attest to their needs for improvement in these basic capacities (46) (64). In general the retardate is from two to four years deficient in tasks requiring strength and/or endurance. The neurologically handicapped child is usually about two years behind his well-functioning brothers.

Strength-Endurance Exercises. It is difficult to separate tasks which develop strength from those which are purported to improve endurance. For example, if a child has the capacity to perform only one push-up, this can be considered a strength task for him. On the other hand, the child who can perform from 30 to 40 push-ups is probably improving his endurance more than his strength. Most tasks, therefore, can be placed somewhere on a strength-endurance continuum, depending upon the number of repetitions the individual performing it can produce.

Evaluating Strength. The concept of a single strength is not quite a sound one upon viewing the experimental literature. Measures of grip strength, for example, rarely correlate with strengths of other muscle groups of the body (27). At the same time measures of moving strength, *i.e.,* lifting a barbell several times in succession, are sometimes not related to a single strength effort measured in pounds exerted against a relatively immobile obstacle (45). Thus to evaluate strength of a child several kinds of movements should be required, at the same time realizing that only with the most sophisticated measuring apparatus can a truly comprehensive evaluation of a child's strength be made.

Shoulder-arm strength-endurance. Not until the average boy is about 12 years of age can he be expected to perform more than one or two pull-ups on a horizontal bar placed higher than his head. Thus less difficult pulling tasks must be attempted in order to assess individual differences below this age. One measure, which is also a training technique, is a stiff-body pull-up in which the feet remain on the ground. This exercise may also be utilized to evaluate the pulling ability of girls.

If a child can perform from 4-6 modified pull-ups keeping his body rigid, he evidences a reasonable amount of pulling strength. Similarly, if a boy can perform 5 stiff-body-push-ups, or a girl can perform 8-10 knee push-ups as shown, their shoulder-girdle pushing strength is about average.

If a child can hold his legs straight at a 45% angle to the ground while lying on his back for 10 seconds and can perform from three to six sit-ups, his abdominal strength meets acceptable standards. Similarly if he can, while lying on his stomach, raise his head, shoulders and arms above the ground, and hold them there for from 6-10 seconds his back muscles are in moderately good condition.

Trunk strength should be assessed by inspecting both the child's ability to sit up, using the abdominal muscle, as well as by evaluating the strength of the large muscles in the small of the back which extend the trunk.

Leg strength may be assessed by evaluating the child's leg power. Power is the combination of both strength and speed, and is best measured by some kind of jumping task. A girl should be able to execute a standing broad jump a distance equal to her height. A boy, on the other hand, should be able to execute a standing broad-jump a distance which is about one foot greater than his height.

Both boys and girls should be able to jump vertically from eight to ten inches higher than they can reach above their heads with their arms fully extended.

Flexibility may be evaluated in a number of ways, and at least two types of measures are utilized: one, to evaluate flexibility of the muscles to the rear of the body, the backs of the legs, hips, etc., and two, to evaluate shoulder-girdle flexibility. Trunk-flexion rear-leg flexibility may be ascertained by asking the child to bend forward and attempt to touch the floor, while keeping his knees straight. If the child can touch his fingertips to the floor, a fair degree of flexibility is indicated. If the palmar surfaces of the hands can be placed on the floor a good degree of flexibility of the muscle groups involved is indicated.

Shoulder-girdle flexibility can be ascertained by asking the child to stand with his back to a wall and with arms extended, level with the shoulders, elbows straight and palms forward; ask him to attempt to touch the backs of both hands to the wall against which he is standing. If the child can accomplish this unusual task, muscular rigidity is probably not present to any marked degree in the shoulder-girdle region.

Thus, if a child can exhibit reasonable back, abdominal, shoulder-girdle strength as well as appropriate leg power after evaluating him on the tests outlined above, specific exercises should be used sparingly, and the emphasis should be placed upon sports skills, and upon tasks which involve necessity for muscle groups to work "in concert." Similarly, if the flexibility tasks are accomplished reasonably well, no specific exercises are probably called for.

Exercise Program. Strength exercises, if performed under some kind of speed stress (how many can you do in 30 seconds?) contribute to a child's endurance. At the same time it should be noted that flexibility exercises should always be performed slowly, with positions held for from four to six seconds, to gain maximum benefits.

The exercises on the following pages are suggestive of innumerable others. Several basic principles should be kept in mind when performing these movements. (1) Strength and endurance may be improved only if the child exerts himself to his fullest capacities; (2) flexibility movements should be performed slowly and deliberately, rather than rapidly and in a "bouncing" manner; (3) several exercises should be utilized in the program, designed to place stress upon most of the body's larger muscle group; (4) exercise programs containing strength-endurance tasks should be placed at the end of the motor education program so that excessive fatigue will not interfere with learning. Stretching movements may be properly placed at the beginning of the class time. (5) Well-motivated exercise programs should give the child a knowledge of his performance as compared to others of similar age and physical-mental classification, and at the same time provide him with graphic descriptions of his progress.

At the same time, most children can utilize to good advantage exercises intended to improve strength-endurance as well as power in some of the larger muscle groups. With a gain in strength-endurance and power, greater capacities to perform vigorous sports movements should be the outcome.

SELECTED STRENGTH EXERCISES

Shoulder-Girdle
Pushing:
Standing wall push

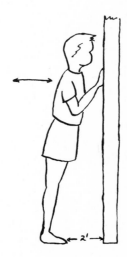

Knee push-up
Feet push-up
Feet raised push-up

Pulling:
    Low-bar pull-up
    Seated to standing rope climb

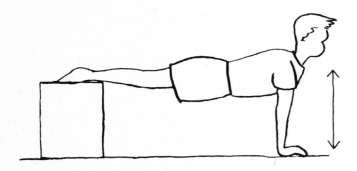

Seated towel-pull in pairs

Reverse sit-up, on stomach

Hi-bar pull-up, feet off ground
Abdominal-lower back:
    Bent body curl-up
    Bent knee leg rotation, upper body fixed

Reverse sit-up, off end of bench, executed slowly

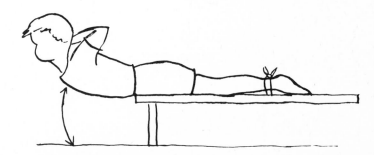

Leg strengtheners:
   Isometric pushing, in back-lying position

Flexibility:
   Sit and slowly reach

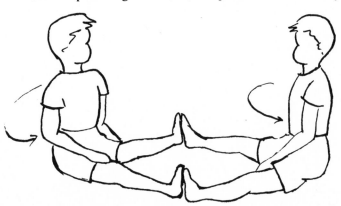

One-half squats to chair, back flat, in pairs

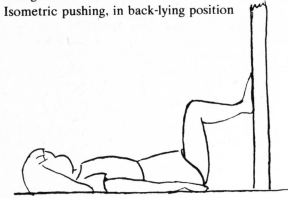

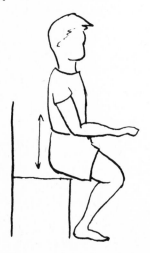

Seated spread-leg stretchers, two persons, rotate slowly

Children may rotate individually as pictured, or may hold each other's wrists (left to right), for a more vigorous stretching action while rotating in unison.

Trunk twisters, touch opposite foot while standing

Cross-leg standing, reach for floor, attempt to touch right toe with left hand, slowly

SUMMARY

Strength, endurance, and flexibility underlie the performance of a number of sports skills. The improvement of these basic attributes is relatively rapid if the child is exposed to planned programs of exercise in which he is gradually "overloaded" and encouraged to extend himself.

Graphic records, as motivational devices, should be kept of the children's progress, as improvement in these qualities is relatively rapid and usually quite apparent to the participants. It should be pointed out to the children that increased fitness contributes in a direct way to their ability to perform a number of physical skills.

Flexibility is best gained with a comprehensive program of slow stretching movements, incorporating exercises involving a number of muscle groups. Strength is improved by the continual application of increased resistance against which the child should be encouraged to work. Endurance is more difficult to gain, and more quickly "lost" than is strength; it may be best improved by presenting the child with tasks which overload his cardio-respiratory system. Running, sustained exercise, and exercises performed within a relatively short time period promote endurance.

CHAPTER IX
CATCHING AND THROWING BALLS

The social success of the growing child within the American culture is partly attributable to his ability to handle balls. A child who cannot adequately track a ball and intercept it with his hands often endures social punishment from his peers. And when this censure is forthcoming, his performance suffers even more upon subsequent confrontations with the elusive missiles as increased tensions begin to interfere with the precise skill required.

The origins for throwing balls is somewhat obscure. Some authorities say that throwing is an inherent kind of defensive skill, a throwback to some early ancestor's need for protection (27). Others suggest that throwing may stem from an accidental arm swing of a child, the resultant centrifugal forces which eject the held object from the palm and the subsequent pleasure derived as the missile hits something and makes a satisfying noise.

Generally there are several stages through which a child passes when learning to throw. First, a simple two-handed push or throw with both arms employed in unison; second, a single-hand throw with no shift of body weight; third, a one-hand throw accompanied by a step of the same leg; and finally, a refined throwing movement seen in the major league baseball player, the single throw with a simultaneous weight shift and step with the opposite foot (27).

Throwing at a target seems to be one of the unique motor skills which only man can accomplish. Our primate ancestors cannot stabilize their bodies well when throwing nor can they coordinate their hands and eyes to the same degree as do humans.

Catching is even a more refined action pattern, necessitating the accurate visual traveling of an object, placing the body in a position to intercept the missile's pathway, and delicately closing the hand upon the arriving spheroid (18) (40) (113). One stands in marvel of the sensitive "computerized mechanisms" that are functioning within the human neuromotor system which permit such an exact perceptual judgment. Needless to say children with impaired nervous systems can be expected to perform these complex skills with less efficiency than do their more fortunate peers (9). Although most retardates and neurologically handicapped children have devised methods of throwing, relatively few can accomplish this with accuracy. Catching poses even more serious problems for the child with perceptual-motor problems. Rarely can a trainable retardate catch a small ball thrown with any velocity from a distance of more than twenty feet (30). The neurologically handicapped child has similar problems when attempting to anticipate the pathways of balls he wishes to intercept.

Relatively little basic information is available concerning the throwing and catching behavior of children. In addition to the four-step breakdown alluded to in the previous paragraph, it is also known that although infants of a few weeks are able to track moving obstacles, it is not until about the age of two years that normal children can be expected to catch a large ball by using both hands (40) (60).

A normal child by the age of six can usually be taught a correct one-handed throw, but he does not intercept small balls well until about the age of eight or nine (27). In a recent investigation it was found that when normal youngsters of five to seven years of age were asked to run to the place they believed a ball would land (they were not permitted to observe the final part of the trajectory) they responded at once, but inaccurately (29). The eight-year-olds in this investigation reacted slower, but began to evidence an awareness of where the ball would really descend. On the other hand, children of nine to eleven reacted both rapidly and accurately when asked to make the same perceptual judgments.

Retarded children and those with minimal neurological impairment evidence considerably less proficiency in these kinds of tasks. For example, in a recent investigation by the author only about 22% of the mongoloid children could catch a large playground ball bounced to them from a distance of ten feet in five out of five attempts. Sixty percent of the trainable retardates could do so five times out of five, where as 90% of the educable retardates could do so. Significant differences were noted when this same task was administrated to a group of children with mild to moderate perceptual-motor handicaps. Only 5% of this latter group were able to catch the large ball in all five trials (30).

When the task is to intercept a smaller missile, children with mental and moderate motor handicaps evidence even more problems. When presented with a standard size softball, suspended and swung on a 15" string (arms distance away), even fewer of the children were able to touch it (30). For example, only 2% of the mongoloids could consistently intercept its pathway, while only 10% of the trainable retardates and only about 27% of the educable retardates and neurologically handicapped children were able to do so (30).

Several research studies indicate, however, that throwing and catching abilities in children are highly trainable. In the study cited above, the mongoloid children evidence regular improvement with age, perhaps indicating the results of parental interest in the development of this kind of skill (30). The training of ball catching, however, must for many children consist of relatively precise steps toward the more complex whole. To subject a child to the social and physical punishment inherent in a ball game in which he is continually experiencing failure teaches him nothing but that he *cannot* accomplish this kind of task.

The Evaluation of Throwing and Catching

Throwing. To evaluate throwing behavior one should ask the child to throw a small ball (diameter about 3"-4") with one hand. If the child is six years or older he should evidence an appropriate weight shift forward as he releases the ball. If the child is asked to throw for about his maximum distance he should be seen to take a step forward with the foot opposite to that of the throwing hand as he shifts his weight forward.

Throwing accuracy may be evaluated by asking the child to throw the ball into a 2' x 2' square placed on the ground about fifteen feet away. Most children should be able to accomplish this at least three out of five times. If the child fails to hit this target even once out of five trials, it is indicative of at least a moderate skill problem.

Catching Proficiency. Balls of two sizes should be utilized to evaluate a child's catching ability. First, a large playground ball (diameter 8") should be bounced to the child so that it arrives chest-high, from a distance of ten feet. The mongoloid child can be expected to catch the ball three out of five times, while most minimally neurologically handicapped children and educable and trainable retardates can intercept it from three to five times out of five.

If the child can catch the larger ball four or five times out of five the smaller ball should be utilized. This may be thrown to the child without a bounce, from a distance of five to six feet.

Normal ability in this latter task on the part of children several years and older are three out of five catches. Older children should do even better. The throw should arrive chest-high, and the arc of the ball should not be higher than the child's head.

The Improvement of Throwing. A child's throwing ability should be practiced from two standpoints; throwing *form*—the means by which the child utilizes his arms, legs, and body in "concert," and the ability to throw at a target. Although these two sub-skills are somewhat related, it is not unusual to see a child who has adopted an immature throwing pattern (*i.e.*, a two-handed overhead throw) do so with accuracy due to extensive practice (30).

Throwing "form" should be accomplished by having the child utilize another child or adult as a model, as well as by practicing in front of a mirror so that he may observe his own movements. Care should be taken to elicit the appropriate weight shift and to throw one-handed when possible. The addition of a foot-print, on which to step with the foot opposite to that of the throwing hand, may be of help. Prior to having the child throw extensively at targets, his form should be molded correctly. Requisite to throwing for accuracy is the ability to watch a point when throwing, rather than having the head and eyes wander in a random manner as the ball or other missile is released.

Throwing for accuracy can be enhanced by first attempting to intercept fixed targets of decreasing size and increasing distance from the thrower (48) (122). Later the child should be encouraged to attempt to hit moving targets. He should be expected to initially hit with most accuracy those moving in the opposite direction, and then those moving laterally away from the thrower (48). Later more difficulty can be achieved by introducing target positions, and laterally toward him.

A final level of difficulty, of course, can be induced by asking the child to move while throwing first at fixed targets and then at moving targets. This latter skill level can only be achieved after extensive practice by children in late childhood and early adolescence.

Neurologically handicapped children who are distractable will evidence difficulty in this kind of task not only because of poor visual-motor coordination, but also because they cannot seem to concentrate their attention on the target at which they are throwing when it is appropriate (33). The instructor should attempt to determine whether a child's inaccuracy is due to inability to coordinate hand with vision, or due to hyperactivity which seems to impedes even looking at the target for sufficient periods of time.

The use of light plastic balls has been shown to heighten a child's sensitivity to the weight of a normal ball when throwing. If a child can hit a target with frequency with the lighter ball, it has been shown that his accuracy when throwing a ball of normal weight will be improved.

Training for Catching. Catching balls is a more difficult task for children than throwing, perhaps because it combines the necessity to make various perceptual-judgments as the ball is visually tracked initially, and the motor problems of getting the body in the proper position, and of closing the hands correctly.

Basic research related to visual tracking indicates that several kinds of situations can improve or impede the chances that an individual will correctly judge the pathway of a moving object. For example, small objects are usually perceived as traveling faster than larger ones, even though both may be traveling at the same speed (27) (122). The speed of objects coming straight at the catcher are more difficult to judge than missiles arriving at an angle from the left or right (27). Objects traveling across intervening lines and objects are more easily judged than are objects traversing space fields in which there are few auxiliary cues (27). Data indicates that the speed of objects descending are more difficult to judge than objects rising (48).

This information has relevance to a program designed to enhance a child's catching ability. For example, balls of several sizes should be thrown to a youngster so that he may make quick judgments to speed and size cues within the situation. Similarly, balls should be thrown high in the air to a child, as the research indicates that these kinds of throws will cause him the most trouble.

Several basic kinds of drills will prepare a child to deal better will balls. For example, rolling the ball on the floor eliminates one of the three dimensions in which a ball can move when approaching, and thus, this drill should enable a child to make the more complex judgments which will be required later.

The use of a ball on a string should also aid a child to learn the judgments necessary when he is later confronted with faster moving balls. This kind of drill presents a problem to the child which involves tracking, but which at the same time will not result in injury if he misses it, as will a ball thrown at him. Similarly, the speed and direction of the swinging missile is more easily modified and more predictable than are the speeds and directions of thrown balls.

A ball the size of a tennis ball or one slightly larger is of sufficient size in this kind of drill.

Initially, the teacher can simply have the child attempt to watch the ball as it is swung on the string. Later the child can be required to touch it with his finger, while the task may be made more difficult later by asking him to touch a particular design which may be placed on a spinning ball suspended on a string.

The order of difficulty suggested for exercises using this kind of swinging ball is as follows:

1. Watching and then attempting to touch or catch a ball swinging directly in front of the child, so that it moves from near to far.

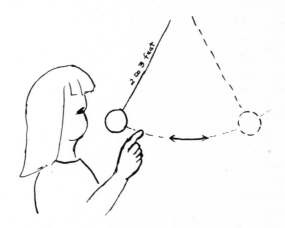

2. Watching and then touching or catching a ball that is swinging from left to right in a line perpendicular to a line passing across the child's shoulders.

3. Watching and then touching or catching a ball that is swinging in a circle in front of the child.

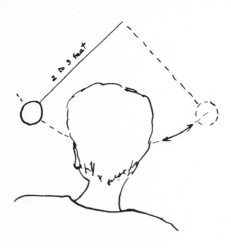

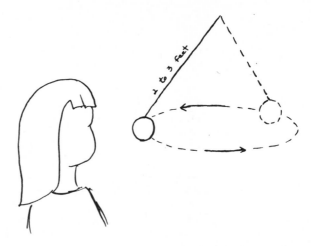

4. Watching, and then attempting to touch or catch a ball that is attached directly above the child and is swung in a large circle completely around him.

The ball's height should be set so that the circumference around which the ball swings is about 20".

5. The child may also be placed in a back-lying position, and observe these balls swinging in various pathways.

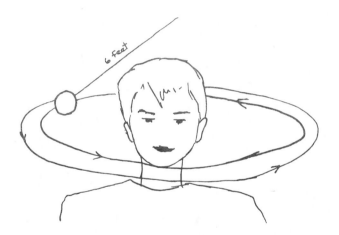

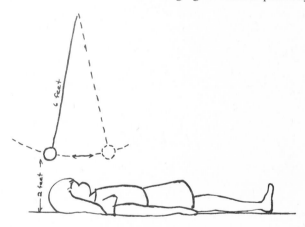

These tasks can be made more difficult by requiring that the child touch a spot on the ball as it is spinning on the string. These exercises can be followed by the usual games of catch. Usually games in which the ball is bounced to the child are easier than those in which contact or a catch must be made while the ball is in the air.

Intercepting Balls with an Extension of the Body.
Numerous games including baseball, tennis, badminton, and paddle tennis involve attempting to intercept a ball with a racket or other implement which is an extension of the body. Usually this is more difficult than merely catching or striking the ball with the hand.

A good lead up sequence to facilitate batting a softball, for example, includes:

1. Striking a ball which is held immobile on batting T.
2. Striking a rolling volleyball on the ground with the bat in a golf-like motion.
3. Striking a volleyball bounced to the batter.
4. Striking a volleyball thrown to the batter.
5. Balls of decreasing size can be used until the child can manage to strike a baseball of the required size.

SUMMARY

Tennis and other games in which a racket is used may be prepared for by first having the child attempt to catch the ball in their hands, and then asking him to strike the balls on a T with the appropriate rackets, and later when suspended from strings as described in the previous paragraphs.

A number of tasks should be used to enhance ball handling skills. The balls should be of a variety of weight and size, and should be thrown from a variety of angles and heights. The child with perceptual-motor problems should be led through gradual steps into the complex skills needed to complete successfully in the ball games deemed important by his peers. Too sudden an exposure to baseball, for example, will so discourage the child, due to a combination of the punishment dealt out by the missed ball and the more subtle punishment dealt to him by his peers, that he may never find the courage and fortitude to compete successfully.

CHAPTER X
MANUAL ABILITIES

The human hand is one of the most precise instruments in existence. It is capable of making fine discriminations in texture (118), or when gripping tools may act with great force (43). The hands throw, catch, and distinguish the differences in the shapes of innumerable objects. The hand is a sensitive barometer to the "emotional tone" of an individual, while at times it becomes a means through which the intellect is expressed, as handwriting and other classroom tasks are engaged in.

The perceptual judgments which the hands make, and the accuracy with which the hands and fingers move, are inseparable. Recent research indicates that there exists an almost perfect correlation between measures evaluating the child's *awareness* of his fingers and the ability to *use* his fingers in precise manual skills (7) (13) (51). Thus any program designed to improve manual ability should incorporate tasks designed to heighten the child's perceptual awareness of the hands and fingers, just as a program to improve gross motor coordination of the large muscles should include activities to heighten the body-image (Chapter III).

It is not unusual to find that children with learning problems are also having difficulty performing various manual and handwriting skills. The reasons for this are several: (1) It is likely that any kind of organic brain damage present in the motor cortex will affect manual skill simply because of the large area within this region which controls the movements of the hands.[1] (2) Children with the ability to perceive their perceptual-motor ineptitudes frequently reflect their concern about themselves in residual muscle tension; and many times the focus of this tension is in the hands. (3) Early and slight ineptitude in the socially prized manual skills confronting a child (eating, tying the shoes, etc.) will frequently become a cause of parental concern and tension which will many times heighten the problem.

Manual dexterity, however, is not a uni-dimensional attribute but in reality is composed of several sub-skills (43). Thus to improve the manual ability of a child several classifications of abilities must be trained.

Although investigations of the manual abilities of *adults* indicate that innumerable factors underlie manual dexterity, it is believed that the manual dexterity of *children* with motor problems is not as complex. At the same time it is believed that training in at least four areas are important to the child whose hands will not perform tasks with the desired efficiency. These areas include tasks involving finger dexterity, hand-eye tracking (writing), steadiness-aiming tasks, and activities designed to heighten the child's perceptions of his hands. Another perceptual attribute of which the hands are capable—the ability to perceive shapes—may also be improved through training.

Evaluating Manual Skill in Children. A child's lack of adequate manual skill is quite apparent to his parents. These children cannot tie their shoes, nor can they handle table utensils with proficiency; they have trouble grasping blocks, and when asked to begin to draw simple lines and letters, they exhibit marked ineptitude.

---

[1] The extent of the area within the motor cortex allotted to given muscular functions is related to the precision with which the muscular systems may move. Thus relatively little area is accorded the large leg muscles, while an extensive area is devoted to the meditation of hand movements, particularly to the thumb and first finger.

Several specific tasks may be utilized, however, to evaluate more exactly the manual skill of children.

(1) Finger opposition: The child may be asked to touch in order, from the first to little finger, each of his fingers to his thumb. The child of four and five will be able to do this with some hesitation, and will need to watch his fingers. He may skip his "ring" finger at times, or have difficulty touching it to his thumb. By the age of six, however, most children will be able to carry out "finger opposition" quite well, and will be able to accomplish this exercise using both hands at the same time or one hand at a time.

By the sixth year most children should be able to oppose all the fingers to the thumb precisely, with their eyes closed or open. Inability to carry out this exercise is usually indicative of mild to moderate dexterity problems. Unusually slow movements or frequent "missing" of fingers by the thumb are signs that the child's abilities to perceive and to control his hands are deficient.

(2) Requiring the child to connect dots with a pencilled line will also reveal problems in visual-manual coordination, and is predictive of future difficulties in handwriting. If the dots are placed about eight inches apart on a page in front of the child, most children by the age of five can connect them with a pencil without undue strain. If the child draws past the second dot, or draws an unusually "shaky" line when approaching the second dot with his pencil, it is usually indicative of deficiencies in handwriting skill, important to early academic success.

(3) Finger dexterity also can be evaluated by asking the child to pick up small objects, *i.e.*, pins, and place them in a match box. By the age of four to five most children can efficiently accomplish this kind of task, and the inability to do so also is usually predictive of problems in precise finger control.

TRAINING SKILLS. As with most motor training the practicing of manual skills should be carried out in as relaxed an environment as possible. The emotionality which accompanies failure frequently centers in the hands, thus producing a "circle" of failure-tension-further failure-etc., which will prove increasingly difficult to overcome.

Tasks in at least two of the following sections should be included in a daily program for a child needing help in these competencies—tasks intended to aid in heightening the perceptions of the hands, and those which involve specific motor problems. The tasks should be incorporated into games when possible. For example, line-drawing can consist of "drawing roads from one house to another."

The practice sessions in these tasks should be frequent and relatively short. When possible a variety of materials intended to improve a single attribute should be employed to aid in motivating the child. For example, in tasks involving finger dexterity, various size and shaped objects might be sorted during a single training session.

The child should be encouraged to watch his hands at work, and to watch the hands of others performing the desired skills. A recent research study found that as much learning was accomplished in a manual skill performed with one hand when a demonstration was watched as when the same skill was first practiced by the subjects with their other hand! (38)

PERCEPTIONS OF THE HANDS. Two kinds of tasks are included in this section—those intended to improve the child's *perceptions of* his hands, and those intended to facilitate his perception *of* things *by* his hands.[2]

Clay Modeling. Relatively unstructured clay modeling should be incorporated into a program of this nature. Clay which is relatively easy to manipulate should be employed, and emphasis should be placed on the activity itself rather than the production of a final product in the form of an artistic ceramic. The child should be encouraged to squeeze the clay between his fingers and to manipulate the clay in every way possible and into many shapes.

Finger Painting. Finger painting is another excellent exercise for heightening the perceptions of the hands and fingers. The child should be encouraged to draw lines and shapes in all directions with his fingers; circles, squares, and slanting and vertical lines should be included in his "painting." Particular emphasis should be placed upon using *all* the fingers in this kind of activity; the fingers may be used separately and in various combinations. Finger painting should be carried out with both the dominant and non-dominant hands. At times, finger painting with the eyes closed may be encouraged.

The Object Box. One technique intended to heighten the child's perceptions of shape consists of a box containing a variety of small objects which the child may feel, but may not see. There are several kinds of exercises which may be engaged in when using such a device. He may be asked to reach in the box and to locate an unseen object which matches an object he is inspecting.[3] He may be asked to simply locate objects described verbally (*i.e.,* "find the triangle"). He may be asked to manipulate objects within the box, and to place them in pairs depending upon various qualities they might possess (*i.e.,* "pair the biggest, the heaviest, the roughest, etc. together").

Fine sensory discrimination may be encouraged with such a device. For example, the child may be asked to arrange, in a row, various shapes according to their weight, size, etc.

---

[2]The technical name for this perceptual quality is *sterognosis.*

[3]Such inter-sensory training is finding more and more applications within education, *i.e.,* the transfer of a perception based upon one kind of sensory input (vision) with a perception depending upon another kind of sensation (*i.e.,* tactile-kinesthetic input).

FINGER-HAND DEXTERITY. Many children lack the ability to handle small objects, and to transfer them from place to place with precision. This attribute depends upon the child's sensitivity to the presence of small objects within the fingers, and also upon hand-eye integration as such objects are lifted and released into receptacles. Finger-hand dexterity underlies a number of manual skills important in industry, including many kinds of assembly tasks. This quality may be improved by engaging in several kinds of tasks.

Match Transfer. Using matches of various sizes the child may be required to take them from one location and transfer them to another, *i.e.,* from one box to another. Increased difficulty may be obtained by decreasing the size of the matches, by decreasing the size of the receptacle into which they are to be placed, and be requiring that the work be carried out with increased speed. Similar tasks using small nuts and bolts may also be employed in this way.

Assembly Tasks. After a reasonable improvement is seen in tasks in the previous category, the child may be given simple assembly tasks to complete, including placing a washer and then a nut on upright bolts, for example. "Speed stress" may also increase the difficulty of this kind of task, as well as decreasing the size of the components of the assembly involved.

AIMING-STEADINESS. Another important component of manual dexterity involves the ability to point, and to aim the finger and hand with precision. Such a quality underlies handwriting, finger-hand dexterity, and typewriting.

Circle Dotting. One helpful kind of exercise to improve this skill component involves placing dots, using a paint-tipped finger or pencil, into circles placed on a paper. The circles can be placed in series, and can be of the same or of dissimilar sizes. Additional difficulty can be incorporated in this kind of task by decreasing the size of the circles,

by placing emphasis on speed (*i.e.,* by attempting to perform rhythmically to a metronome), and/or by placing the circles to be dotted increasing distances from one another. The teacher or parent can, through the use of ditto stencils produce pages which present the child with various degrees of difficulty. An example of these are on the pages which follow.

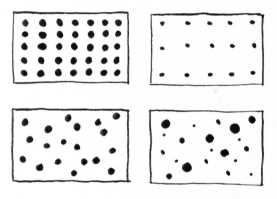

The circles on these pages may be solid as pictured, or in the form of small circles 0...0...etc.

HAND-EYE TRACKING. It is obvious that one of more important manual skills involves the ability to control continuous hand movements while drawing lines of varying complexity. This attribute, of course, is basic to handwriting. The early detection of difficulties in this kind of task together with the institution of proper training procedures can help to by-pass later problems in school. There are several kinds of tasks which can be employed to improve this basic attribute — those involving somewhat structured continuous movements made between guide lines, and relatively unstructured movements from one point on the page to another.

Both of these kinds of tasks can be made more difficult by requiring that the child move with more precision (*i.e.,* draw between narrower guidelines), by requiring that he move through a larger amount of space (*i.e.,* draw a line between dots placed on either side of the page), by requiring that he perform such movements with increasing speed, and by requiring that such movements be made increasingly complex (*i.e.,* drawing between guidelines which require that a half-circle connected to a straight line be made, instead of a simple straight line.

Channel-Drawing. "Channels" in the form of parallel lines may be drawn on pages and then the child may be required to draw with accuracy between them. These guidelines should at first be relatively simple and be placed about one-half inch apart. Initially they should be placed so that they are located directly in front of the child. The child should be asked to draw lines within these guides, from left right, away from and toward his body. More difficult is the drawing of transverse lines, starting from upper right to lower left, from upper left on the page to lower right, etc.

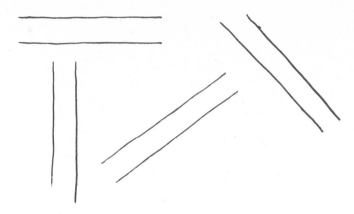

After straight lines are drawn in this manner, and after the distance between the guidelines has been decreased to about 1/8th of an inch the child may be presented with the problem of drawing the more difficult curved lines, placed in various positions around the page.

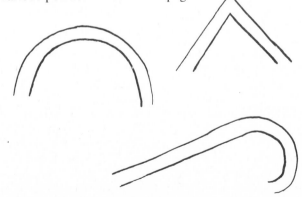

Later compound shapes may be required, including guidelines which include both curves and straight segments in various combinations as in the examples below.

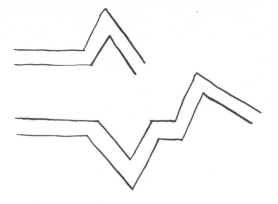

These guides, of course, can be later modified into the shape of letters.

Dot-Connecting. Another type of exercise intended to improve hand-eye tracking involves less structured tasks. Dots may be placed on the page in various ways which encourage the child to make horizontal, then vertical, and then lateral movements as he attempts to connect them. Initially the problem should involve dots rather closely spaced (from two to six inches apart) and placed directly in front of the child, slightly nearer his dominant hand. Later the dots may be separated by greater distances and the child required to cross the midline of his body, a task frequently causing neurologically handicapped children great difficulty.

After these initial exercises have been accomplished the dots may be placed next to various "objects" on the page, with the task to start from a dot, draw around an object and then return to the starting point. Increasing complexity can be achieved as in the examples below, by incorporating more than one "obstacle" to negotiate.

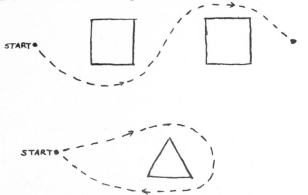

The dots and obstacles may be arranged later so that connecting them will produce various block letters as well as cursive letters, as in the examples below.

SUMMARY

Manual dexterity depends upon the child's perceptions of his hands as well as his ability to control their movements in a variety of tasks. Thus training in manual skill should incorporate tasks designed to enhance several kinds of attributes, including hand-finger perception, finger-hand dexterity, shape-recognition, hand-eye tracking, and aiming-steadiness.

The training should be well motivated, relatively brief in duration each day, and consist of several kinds of tasks designed to improve the various factors of manual dexterity. Emphasis should be upon the employment of reasonable, orderly sequences of activities of increasing difficulty as indicated on the previous pages. Tasks designed to heighten manual dexterity can be made increasingly difficult by requiring that they be performed with increased speed, with increased precision (*i.e.,* involving finer discriminations in space), and/or by requiring that the child work at the periphery rather than at the central part of his desk.

CHAPTER XI
MOVING AND THINKING

Movements are usually accompanied to some degree by thought. With the exception of a reflexive withdrawal of the hand from a hot stove, most human actions are either preceded by, accompanied by, or followed by cognition.

In the preceding chapters innumerable connections have been drawn between thought processes and movement. For example, gaining of the concept of laterality in children may be enhanced by movement activities; raising one's left hand when asked may be in the final analysis evidence of concept rather than a simple motor act. In the chapter concerned with manual activity, it is emphasized that many manual skills are important because they are the primary means by which one may evidence intellectual functioning.

Human behavior is often classified into three or four components consisting of motor activity, the formation of perceptions, verbal behavior, and concept formation. These behaviors are not mutually exclusive. Motor behavior, however, is the primary channel through which evidence of the other behaviors is apparent to others. Thus motor activity is the observable evidence of the extent to which the higher thought processes may or may not be functioning properly. The quality of a child's decision making, perceptual organization of time and space, and categorizing may thus be "acted out" through movement. Movement experiences may thus serve as an important modality through which a child may learn (67) (80) (84).

But learning and thinking are not singular activities. One learns how to learn. We learn how to organize material, to memorize concepts, to keep focused on a task, and to organize spatial and quantitative concepts. Psychologists speak of acquiring learning "sets" or predispositions for mastering certain classifications of tasks (39).

It is proposed in this chapter to offer examples of three components of the learning process which may be enhanced through motor activity. Gross activity is a sensory experience in which the child is *totally* involved; his vision, his kinesthetic input, vestibular cues, and tactile experiences combine to produce a meaningful experience which can be used to produce more effective, more motivating, and quicker classroom learning on the part of retarded and neurologically handicapped children.

The types of learning outlined in this section include tasks purporting to aid pattern recognition, activities to enhance serial memory ability, and tasks which may aid in lengthening the attention span. Other components of the learning process may also be approached in a similar way, including decision making, creative thinking and the like (67) (84). It is certain that motor-thinking relationships will occur to the reader as he begins to concern himself more about components of cognition while reading these pages.

Pattern Recognition. The child with the defective nervous system as well as the immature child in our highly verbal society ultimately must face the problem of learning to read. But prior to reading one must recognize words, and prior to this the child must identify letters. Even more basic than this is the need to recognize the few simple geometric shapes which combine in various ways to form letters.

If one surveys the shapes on the playground to which the child is usually exposed, he will find the expected squares and circles. Children play base games in squares or perhaps dodge ball on a circle, but rarely do they find themselves playing games on triangles, half-circles, or rectangles.

If one accepts the premise that gross movement is another helpful modality through which one may learn, it is also reasonable to assume that placing these other shapes on the playground and encouraging children to walk around them, to talk about them, and to play games on them, may help them to learn these shapes when they appear in other forms on the blackboard and in books (31).

Such transfer must be taught, however (39). Children with learning problems cannot be expected to somehow assimilate these spatial concepts without careful planning on the part of the teacher. It is believed that several steps must be taken when attempting to utilize gross movement in this way. These steps are not mutually exclusive but should overlap in time.

1. Initially, drill should take place in a classroom concerning what are the components of triangles, half-circles squares, and rectangles. They should be talked about, drawn on the blackboard, and the shapes should be handled.

2. Secondly, the children should go to the playground and attempt to find these shapes, walk around them, and discuss such qualities as the number of sides, etc. Practice of this kind can take place as they hold the shapes utilized in the classroom in their hands.

Further experiences could include playing games in utilizing these shapes, practicing agility exercises around their periphery, and the like. The children may also be asked to walk through various patterns in a sandbox, and then to visually inspect the pathways they transcribed with their footprints.

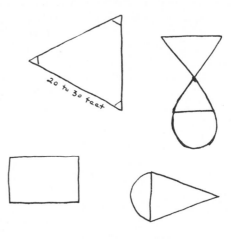

3. Third, the children could begin to determine in the classroom how certain shapes are modifiable into letters; triangles can become A's, two half-circles become a B, etc.

4. Following this a final step could include finding these same letters on the playground. Games can be played on a Z, while other letters could be utilized in the same way as were the more simple shapes to which the children were initially exposed.

It is not assumed that this method could constitute the sole approach to pattern and letter recognition; however, for children with learning problems, it is believed that it presents another helpful avenue which can be traveled in a quest for clearer understanding.

Serial Memory Ability. If a child is asked to learn a series of movements, his learning curve will evidence many of the same characteristics as it would if he were asked to learn a series of words (32). First he will acquire the initial movements in the series; secondly, the final portions of the series; and last, the middle portions. The available evidence indicates that the serial learning of movements is quite similar to the correct placing and learning of words or ideas in a series (32).

If a child cannot remember to execute two observable movements in correct series, it is probably more than can be expected if he is asked to remember that to spell "no" one must first place an "n" and then an "o." However, the reasons for his confusion while spelling is rarely discernable as his eyes flick across the printed page.

Memory for a series of things is sometimes called our perceptual span, a concept painful to many of us when the telephone company recently changed to digit dialing (27). Although not entirely similar to the concept of serial memory necessary in spelling, it is believed that both components of the learning process may be enhanced by requiring a child to remember increasingly complex series of movements as found, for example, in an obstacle course.

First a child may be asked to walk a line. For some seriously disturbed youngsters this is a formidable feat! Next he may be asked to walk the line and then jump into a small circle at the end of the line. If the child can accomplish this, and thus evidence the ability to remember two related acts in a series, additional components may be added until the child becomes able to remember increasingly long lists of things, and to place them in a correct order. Serial memory can be enhanced directly in spelling tasks through gross movement by asking them to jump into girded squares into which letters have been placed.

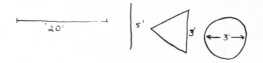

It is as yet unclear how helpful this technique may be in the process of spelling; however, it is difficult to conceive of how a child can remember that *cat* is spelled with three letters in a given order, if he cannot organize three gross movements in the correct series.

"Focusing" the Hyperactive Child. One of the most difficult enigmas to deal with in the educational setting is the hyperactive, distractable child (33). This child cannot synthesize and organize experience because he rarely stops to consider minutia. He has difficulty seeing objects in complex backgrounds because he rarely focuses upon anything *but* the background.

Motorically the hyperactive child is quite different from the "normal" youngster and rarely pauses to engage in purposeful activity, spending the majority of his time in seemingly random exploratory, manipulatory behavior.

A recent investigation with normal children demonstrated the importance of motoric control to learning. A significant positive correlation was obtained between intellectual measures and the performances which required that the children perform such tasks as drawing lines as slowly as possible, walking as slowly as they could, etc. (80).

If the motor activities of hyperactive children are somehow physically restrained, he is visually seen to engage in hyperactive "behavior," rarely focusing his eyes on a single component of his environment for more than a few seconds. The interference of this kind of behavior with the learning processes is apparent. If one is to learn about something, he must look at it and consider it for increasingly longer periods of time, something that the hyperactive child fails to do (80).

It is believed that through purposeful, well-controlled motor activity, such a child may be directed into assuming self-control to increasing degrees. In environments which are relatively distraction-free such a child can be directed in an interesting motor task (*i.e.,* walking a balance beam) and be motivated to persist in this task, partly because he may fear the consequences of failure, *i.e.,* falling off the beam, and partly because there is simply nothing else to do or to look at. After the child has seemingly acquired the ability to walk a beam for 15 seconds (perhaps a period of time longer than he has even concentrated upon anything before) a longer beam or a more lengthy task may be utilized.

It is important to demand that hyperactive children attempt to "stretch" their attention span slightly longer than they would normally be willing to do so, and to reward them when they do. Similarly, one must be alert to the fact that when such a child has mastered a motor task of this nature and seemingly continues to concentrate upon its execution, he may, in truth, be preoccupied visually with other stimuli while motorically carrying out the wishes of the teacher.

Using this technique the author has lengthened the clocked attention span of children from 5-10 seconds to several minutes. The extent to which this transfers to classroom learning is unclear at this time; however, if one is able, through such planned motor activity, to engage a child in tasks longer than he has ever been constructively occupied, it would seem that this improved attention span should merge in the classroom.

Innumerable tasks can help a retarded and neurologically handicapped child think with more efficiency. After being given ways of walking a balance beam, for example, a teacher might ask such a child to think of ways he may do it. The usual pause and hesitation should be a hopeful sign, for during this apparently inactive period the child is thinking—and what could be more attractive behavior in a so-called retarded child?

With proper guidance such a child could explore what balance is as he attempts to assume stable and unstable positions. Similarly, creative thinking can be promoted as the child is presented with a rope, a stick, and a ball that doesn't roll very well, and then asked to invent games. The ideas and uses of movement as a learning modality are limited only by the creative energy and thinking ability of the teacher.

CHAPTER XII
SUMMARY AND PROGRAM SUGGESTIONS

The activities on the preceding pages represent sequences through which the perceptual-motor attributes of retarded and neurologically handicapped children may be improved. These sequences are intended to be representative of many such tasks through which the movement capacities of atypical children can be enhanced.

It has been assumed that improvement in motor ability will aid the child to function better in a social context, and at the same time will contribute in a direct way to certain components of classroom learning. Most child development experts emphasize the importance of the sensory-motor period occuring early in the infant's life span. Frequently children with learning problems evidence developmental gaps reflected in atypical perceptual-motor behavior, which if rectified may form a sound base from which more complex perceptual judgments necessary in the classroom may be acquired.

The text has outlined numerous categories into which activities have been placed, in so far as the experimental literature indicates that human beings function in rather specific ways. At the same time it has been assumed that certain kinds of transfer of training will be evidenced as a result of engaging in these sequences. For example, the transfer of practice in tasks intended to enhance body-perception should transfer to the child's ability to make various spatial discriminations. The transfer of pattern recognition from the playground to the classroom is also hypothesized in Chapter XI.

Important to the correct use of the sequences presented are the evaluative procedures at the beginning of each chapter. Rather than outlining formulae for certain types of children, it is hoped that the teachers utilizing these materials will first evaluate the children in their charge, and then select sequences, and activities within sequences, appropriate to the abilities of the individual children it is hoped to improve.

For optimum benefit from this kind of training with retardates, and the neurologically handicapped, from 30 minutes to one hour a day (preferably in two 30-minute sessions) should be devoted to activities which are primarily motor in nature (balance, agility, locomotor activities and the like), with another 30 to 45 minutes devoted to the acquisition of classroom concepts utilizing gross movement as a learning modality.

Children within the following categories should be exposed to the sequences indicated. A model schedule for each type of child is indicated on the pages which follow. Practice of some activities may overlap. For example pattern recognition, and moving around and into shapes on the playground may be combined with agility training. Similarly most tumbling and balancing activities may have practice in laterality training incorporated into them. In most cases practice in the various categories of activities, can with a reasonable amount of creative thinking on the part of the teacher, be made mutually complementary. The programs outlined below assume that the children are engaged in a five-day-a-week program in school, with two 30-minute sessions, morning and afternoon, devoted to perceptual-motor activities. It has been assumed that recreational games are independent of these activities.

		MORNING	**AFTERNOON**
Mongoloids	MWF	Agility-Locomotor-Balance	Body-Perception-Manual Training
	TTh	Balance-Body-Perception Practice with Balls	Manual Training Fitness Exercises
Trainable Retardates	MWF	Pattern-Recognition Serial Memory Tasks Balance	Agility-Locomotion Fitness Exercises
	TTh	Manual Training Body-Perception Practice with Balls	Manual Training Body-Perception
Educable Retardates	MWF	Serial Memory Tasks Balance-Agility Body Perception	Manual Training Fitness Exercises
	TTh	Balance-Agility Body-Perception	Manual Training Balls
Neurologically Handicapped	MWF	Locomotion Agility-Balance	Body-Perception Manual Training
	TTh	Fitness Exercises Ball Practice	Manual Training Balance

Although the programs outlined in the previous chapters and in the schedule above contain no reference to specific games appropriate to the children under consideration, there are numerous materials of this nature available (15) (42) (47) (64) (67) (84).

Two kinds of records should be maintained—those designed to motivate the children to further effort, in the form of charts and graphs indicating improvement in fitness scores and the like, and records involving more subtle performance and observational changes based upon performances in balance, agility, and body-perception tests.

The teacher should be sensitive to the social setting in which the activities are carried out (28). Arrangements should be made when possible to work with groups of manageable size, including children of reasonably similar abilities. In addition, care should be taken that the participants are not subjected to scorn from their peers when their efforts are obviously not successful. Such social punishment can greatly retard the learning of motor skills, and has a demonstrable effect upon the fitness and motor ability of atypical children (74) (78) (100) (108) (120).

The materials contained in the text are not intended to be an exhaustive list of tasks with which to improve the perceptual-motor attributes of atypical children. It is hoped therefore that the content of the preceding pages will inspire the scholarly reader to delve into the literature and arrive at his own conclusions concerning the theoretical and practical bases of perceptual-motor functioning. The bibliography at the conclusion of the text also provides a list of sources in which materials may be found which will supply many practical answers to the movement problems of children in the form of lead-up games and similar activities.

GLOSSARY

Body Image: The total perception the child and adult form of their body, including its movement capabilities, shape, size, etc.

Cross-Extension Pattern: The typical arm-leg pattern seen in normal walking crawling and similar behavior consisting of a simultaneous movement to the front of the arm and leg on opposite sides, i.e. touching the left knee and right hand to the ground at the same time when crawling.

Developmental Sequences of Tasks: A series of tasks designed to roughly approximate the order in which such acts might be acquired by the maturing child.

Down's Syndrome: Mongolism; named after Dr. Landen-Down, who first identified the traits accompanying this condition in children.

"Drainage Theory": The theory that physical activities are useful in the draining of excess energies in children.

Dynamic Balance: The ability to maintain equilibrium while engaging in various moving balance tasks, i.e. balance beam walking.

Educable Retardate: Children with an I.Q. from 60-70, usually able to benefit from academic work, but at levels well below that expected of children their age.

Educationally Handicapped: Children with learning problems, having normal I.Q.'s from 70 to 120 or higher, caused by emotional, structural and/or environmental factors. From 50 to 75% of such children usually evidence mild to moderate perceptual-motor problems.

Flexibility, Muscular: The ability to move a limb or limbs through a range of motion. Flexibility is usually measured in degrees, using a joint as the fulcrum.

Flexibility, Perceptual: The ability to quickly change judgments and to move in a variety of ways.

Gross Agility: The ability to integrate body parts quickly and accurately while remaining relatively fixed in space, i.e. getting up and down quickly.

In-Put, Out-Put: Reference to the fact that "in-put" (the individual's perceptions of his movements and of visual space) influences "out-put" (his movement).

Laterality: The conscious awareness on the part of the child that one side of his body differs from the other, and that one is called "left," the other "right," that one can move and can locate oneself relative to these two sides.

Locomotion: Motor behavior which permits us to move from one place to another, including crawling, walking, skipping, etc.

Locomotor Agility: Hopping, Jumping, and other locomotor behavior performed with accuracy and/or speed.

Neurologically Handicapped:	In the context used in the pages of the text a neurologically handicapped child is one who evidences minimal impairment of neuromotor functioning.
Perception:	The process of interpreting sensory information, the integration and organization of stimuli received from various sensory end organs.
Perceptual-Motor:	Reasonably complex voluntary movements involving the combining of sensory information and cues gained from the movement itself into an integrated task may be said to be perceptual-motor act.
Reflex:	Involuntary movements produced by discrete stimuli. The reflexes dealt with in the text are defined as deep tendon reflexes.
Serial Memory Ability:	The ability to remember a series of things, of letters in a word, or of words in a phrase, or of a series of movements within a skill, or a series of skills within a game.
Static Balance:	Balance involving relatively static postural adjustment, i.e. standing or kneeling balances.
Syndrome:	A constellation of relatively stable symptoms indicative of a given disease, type of neurological impairment, or of mental retardation.
Tracking Behavior:	The watching of a moving object, attempting to organize its velocity, direction, etc.
Trainable Retardate:	A child with an I.Q. of from 30-50. Such a child is usually in programs emphasizing self-care skills, social skills, etc., rather than academic work.

BIBLIOGRAPHY

1. Abercrombie, M.L.J.; Gardiner, P.A.; Hansen, E.; Jonckheere, J.; Lindon, R.L.; Solomon, G.; Tyson, M.C.,"Visual, Perceptual and Visuomotor Impairment in Physically Handicapped Children," *Percept. & Mot. Skills,* Monograph Supplement 3-V18, 1964.

2. Abercrombie, M.L.J. and Tyson, M.C., "Body Image and Draw-a-Man Test in Cerebral Palsey," *Develop. Medicine and Child Neurology,* 8, 9-15, 1966.

3. American Association for Health, Physical Education, and Recreation, Bibliography on Research in Psychomotor Function, Physical Education, and Recreation for the Mentally Retarded, 1-36, Oct. 20, 1966.

4. American Association for Health, Physical Education, and Recreation, "Activity Programs for the Mentally Retarded," *Journal of Health, Phys. Ed., Recreation,* April 1966.

5. Ammons, R.B., "Le Mouvement," *Current Psych. Issues,* Georgene H. Seward and John P. Seward (Eds.), Henry Holt & Co., 1958.

6. Auxter, David M., "Strength and Flexibility of Differentially Diagnosed Educable Mentally Retarded Boys," *Res. Quart.,* 37, 455-461, 1966.

7. Ayres, A. Jean, "Perceptual-Motor Dysfunction in Children," Monograph from the Greater Cincinnati District Ohio Occupational Therapy Association Conference, 1-23, 1964.

8. Ayres, A. Jean, "Occupational Therapy for Motor Disorders Resulting from Impairment of the Central Nervous System," *Rehab. Lit.* 21, DR-27, 302-310, 1960.

9. Ayres, A. Jean, "The Role of Gross Motor Activities in the Training of Children with Visual-Motor Retardation," *J. Amer. Optometric Assoc.,* 1961.

10. Barsh, Ray H., "A Movigenic Curriculum," Bulletin No. 25, University of Wisconsin, Madison, Wisconsin, 1965.

11. Bayley, Nancy, "The Development of Motor Abilities, During the First Three Years," Monograph for the Society for Research in Child Development, Washington, D.C., 1935.

12. Bendig, A.W., "Factor Analytic Scales of Need Achievement," *The J. of Gen. Psych.,* 90, 59-67, 1964.

13. Benton, Arthur L., *Right-Left Discrimination and Finger Localization,* New York: Hoeber-Harper, 1959.

14. Berges, J. and Lezine, I., *The Imitation of Gestures,* Suffolk: The Lavenham Press Ltd., 1963.

15. Blake, O. William, and Volpe, Anne M., *Lead-Up Games to Team Sports,* Englewood Cliffs, New Jersey, Prentice-Hall, Inc., 1964.

16. Blane, Howard T., "Space Perception Among Unilaterally Paralyzed Children and Adolescents," *J. of Exp. Psych.,* 63, 244-247, 1959.

17. Bolideau, Edward A. and Levy, C. Michael, "Long-Term Memory as a Function of Retention Time and Other Conditions of Training," *Psych. Rev.,* 71, 27-41, 1964.

18. Brown, V., "Thresholds for Visual Movement," *Psych. Forsch.,* 14, 249-268, 1931.

19. Brown, Robert H., "Visual Sensitivity to Differences in Velocity," *Psych. Bull.,* 58, 89-101, 1961.

20. Bruner, Jerome S., *Toward a Therapy of Instruction,* Cambridge, Mass.: Harvard U. Press, 1966.

21. Burg, Albert and Slade, Hubert, Dynamic Visual Acuity as Related to Age, Sex, and Static Acuity," *J. Appl. Psych.,* 45, 111-116, 1961.

22. Cantrell, Robert Paul, "Body Balance Activity and Perception," *Percept. & Mot. Skills,* 17, 431-437, 1963.

23. Clarke, A.D.B. and Cookson, Margaret, "Perceptual-Motor Transfer in Imbeciles: A Second Series of Experiments," *Brit. J. Psych.,* 53, 321-330, 1962.

24. Corder, W.D., "Effects of Physical Education on the Intellectual, Physical and Social Development of Educable Mentally Retarded Boys," Unpublished Special Project, Nashville, Tennessee: George Peabody College, 1965.

25. Cortes, John B. and Gath, Florence M., "Physique and Self-Description of Temperament," *J. Consult. Psych.,* 29, 432-439, 1965.

26. Coville, Francis H., "The Learning of Motor Skills as Influenced by Knowledge of Mechanical Principles," *J. Ed. Psych.,* 48, 321-327, 1957.

27. Cratty, Bryant, J., *Movement Behavior and Motor Learning,* 2nd Edition, Lea and Fiebger, Philadelphia, 1967.

28. Cratty, Bryant J., *Social Dimensions of Physical Activity,* Englewood Cliffs, New Jersey: Prentice-Hall, Inc., 1967.

29. Cratty, Bryant J., *Psychology and Physical Activity,* Englewood Cliffs, New Jersey: Prentice-Hall, Inc., 1968.

30. Cratty, Bryant J., "The Perceptual-Motor Attributes of Mentally Retarded Children and Youth," Monograph, Mental Retardation Services Board of Los Angeles County, August, 1966.

31. Cratty, Bryant J., "The Influence of Small-Pattern Practice Upon Large-Pattern Learning," *Res. Quart.,* 33, 523-535, 1962.

32. Cratty, Bryant J., "Recency vs. Primacy in a Complex Gross Motor Task," *Res. Quart.,* 34, 3-8, 1963.

33. Cruickshank, William M.; Bentzen, Frances A.; Ratzeburg, Frederick H.; and Tannhauser, Miriam T., *A Teaching Method for Brain-Injured and Hyperactive Children,* Syracuse University Press, 1961.

34. Cumbee, Frances, "A Factorial Analysis of Motor Coordination," *Res. Quart.,* 25, 412-420, 1954.

35. Delacato, Carl H., *The Diagnosis and Treatment of Speech and Reading Problems,* Springfield, Illinois: Charles C. Thomas, 1963.

36. Dawson, William W. and Edwards, R.W., "Motor Development of Retarded Children," *Percept. & Mot. Skills,* 21, 223-226, 1965.

37. Domez, Richard G.; Duckworth, James E.; and Morandi, Anthony J., "Taxonomies and Correlates of Physique," *Psych. Bull.,* 62, 411-426, 1964.

38. Eberhard, Ulrich, "Transfer of Training Related to Finger Dexterity," *Percept. & Mot. Skills,* 17, 274, 1963.

39. Ellis, Henry, *The Transfer of Learning,* New York: The Macmillan Co., 1965.

40. Epstein, William, "Experimental Investigations of the Genesis of Visual Space Perception," *Psych. Bull.,* 61, 115-118, 1964.

41. Fait, Hollis F., *Special Physical Education: Adapted, Corrective, Developmental,* Philadelphia: W.B. Saunders Co., 1966.

42. Fait, Hollis F. and Kupferer, H.J., "A Study of Two Motor Achievement Tests and Their Implications in Planning Physical Education Activities for the Mentally Retarded," *American J. Mental Deficiency,* 60:4, 729-732, 1956.

43. Fleishman, Edwin A. and Ellison, Gaylor D., "A Factor Analysis of Fine Manipulative Tests, *J. Appl. Psych.,* 46, 96-105, 1962.

44. Fleishman, Edwin A. and Hempel, "Factorial Analysis of Complex Psychomotor Performance and Related Skills, *J. Appl. Psych.,* 40, 2, 1956.

45. Fleishman, Edwin A.; Thomas, Paul, and Munroe, Philip, The Dimensions of Physical Fitness — A Factor Analysis of Speed Flexibility, Balance, and Coordination Tests, Technical Report No. 3, Office of Naval Research Department of Industrial Administration and Department of Psychology, New Haven, Conn.: Yale University, September, 1961.

46. Francis, R.J. and Rarick, G.L., Motor Characteristics of the Mentally Retarded, U.S. Office of Education Cooperative Research Project No. 152 (6432), University of Wisconsin, September 16, 1957.

47. Franklin, C.C., Diversified Games and Activities of Low Organization for Mentally Retarded Children, Monograph, Carbondale, Illinois, Southern Illinois University.

48. Gemelli, A., "The Visual Perception of Objective Motion and Subjective Movement," *Psych. Rev.,* 61, 304-314, 1954.

49. Gesell, Arnold and Amatruda, Catherine S., *Developmental Diagnosis,* New York: P.B. Hoeber, Inc., 1960.

50. Getman, G.N., *How to Develop Your Child's Intelligence,* 6th Edition, Announcers Press, Luverne, Minn., 1962.   •

51. Ghent, Lila, "Developmental Changes in Tactual Thresholds on Dominant and Non-dominant Sides," *J. of Comp. and Physio. Psych.,* 54, 670-673, 1961.

52. Glickman, Stephen E., "Perserverative Neural Process and Consolidation of the Memory Trace," *Psych. Bull.,* 58, 218-233, 1961.

53. Gordon, Sol and Golub, Risa S., *Recreation and Socialization for the Brain-Injured Child,* New Jersey Assoc. for Brain-Injured Children, New Jersey, 1966.

54. Goldstein, Jacob and Weiner, Charles, "On Some Relations Between the Perception of Depth and of Movement," *J. of Psych.,* 55, 3-23, 1963.

55. Goodenough, F.L. and Smart, R.C., "Inter-relationships of Motor Abilities in Young Children," *Child Dev.,* 6, 141-153, 1935.

56. Gootsdanker, Robert; Frich, James W.; and Lockhard, Robert B., "Identifying the Acceleration of Visual Targets," *Brit. J. of Psych.,* 52, 1, 31-42, 1961.

57. Gutteridge, Mary V., "A Study of Motor Achievements of Young Children, *Arch. Psych.*, 224, 1939.

58. Guyette, Anna; Wapner, Seymour; Worner, Henry; and Davidson, John, "Some Aspects of Space Perception in Mental Retardates, *Amer. J. of Mental Deficiency,* 69, 90-100, 1964.

59. Hackett, Layne C. and Jenson, Robert G., *A Guide to Movement Exploration,* Palo Alto, Calif.: Peek Publications, 1966.

60. Haith, Marshall M., "The Responses of the Human Newborn to Visual Movement," *J. Exp. Child Psych.,* 3, 235-243, 1966.

61. Harmon, Darell Boyd, *Winter Haven Study of Perceptual Learning.* Winter Haven Lions Research Foundation, Inc., Winter Haven Club, Winter Haven, Fla., 1962.

62. Harmon, Darell Boyd, *Notes on a Dynamic Theory of Vision,* Vol. 1, published by author, 1958.

63. Haskins, Mary Jane, "Development of a Response Recognition Training Film in Tennis, *Percept. & Mot. Skills,* 21, 207-211, 1965.

64. Hayden, Frank J., *Physical Fitness for the Mentally Retarded,* London, Ontario, Canada: University of Western Ontario, Frank Hayden, 1964.

65. Hayden, Frank J., "The Nature of Physical Performance in the Trainable Retarded, Presented at the Joseph P. Kennedy Jr. Foundation, Third International Scientific Symposium on Mental Retardation, Boston, Mass., April 11, 1966.

66. Howe, C., "A Comparison of Motor Skills of Mentally Retarded and Normal Children," *Exceptional Children,* 175, 959-961, 1961.

67. Humphrey, James H., "Comparison of the Use of Active Games and Language Workbook Exercises as Learning Media in the Development of Language Understanding with Third Grade Children, *Percept. & Mot. Skills,* 21, 23-26, 1965.

68. Jones, Mary C., "Psychological Correlates of Somatic Development," *Child Dev.,* 33, 899-911, 1965.

69. Jones, Wayne R. and Ellis, Norman R., "Inhibitory Potential in Rotary Pursuit Acquisition by Normal and Defective Subjects, *J. Exp. Child Psych.,* 6, 534-537.

70. Keogh, Jack, *Motor Performance of Elementary School Children,* Monograph, Department of Physical Education, University of California, Los Angeles, 1965.

71. Kephart, Newell C., *The Slower Learner in the Classroom,* Columbus, Ohio: Charles E. Merrill Books, Inc.

72. Knapp, B., *Skill in Sport: The Attainment of Proficiency,* London: Routledge & Kegan Paul, 1964.

73. Koonce, Jefferson M.; Chambliss, Davis J.; and Irion, Arthur, "Long-Term Reminiscence in the Pursuit Rotor Habit," *J. Exp. Psych.,* 67, 498-500, 1964.

74. Latane, Biff and Arrowood, A. John, "Emotional Arousal and Task Performance," *J. of Appl. Psych.,* 47, 324-327, 1963.

75. Lavery, J.J., "Retention of a Skill Following Training with and without Instruction to Retain," *Percept. & Mot. Skills,* 18, 275-281, 1964.

76. Leton, Donald A., "Visual-Motor Capacities and Ocular Efficiency in Reading," *Percept. & Mot. Skills,* 15, 407-432, 1962.

77. Leibowitz, H.W. and Lomont, J.F., *The Effect of Grid Lines in the Field of View Upon Perception of Motion,* Technical Report #54-201, March, 1954, Wright-Patterson Air Force Base.

78. Locke, Edwin A., "The Relationship of Task Success to Task Likes and Satisfaction," *J. of Appl. Psych.,* 5, 379-385, 1965.

79. MacArthur, R.S., "The Experimental Investigation of Persistence in Secondary School Boys," *Canadian J. of Psych.,* 9, 42-54, 1955.

80. MacCoby, Eleanor E.; Dowley, Edith M.; and Hagen, John W., "Activity Level and Intellectual Functioning in Normal Pre-School Children," *Child. Dev.,* 36, 761-769, 1965.

81. Malpass, L.F., "Motor Proficiency in Institutionalized and Non-Institutionalized Retarded Children and Normal Children," *Amer. J. of Mental Deficiency,* 64:6, 1012-1015, May 1960.

82. Mendel, Giseld, "Children's Preference for Differing Degrees of Novelty," *Child. Dev.,* 36, 452-464, 1966.

83. Mendryk, Stephen, "Reaction Time, Movement Time, and Task Specificity Relationships at Ages 12, 22, 48 Years," *Res. Quart.,* 31, 156-162, 1960.

84. Mosston, Muska, *Teaching Physical Education: From Command to Discovery,* Columbus, Ohio: Charles E. Merrill Books, Inc., 1966.

85. Mosston, Muska, *Developmental Movement,* Columbus, Ohio: Charles E. Merrill Books, Inc., 1965.

86. Naylor, James C. and Briggs, George E., *Long-Term Retention of Learned Skills, a Review of the Literature,* Laboratory of Aviation Psychology, Ohio State University and Ohio State University Research Foundation, August 1961.

87. Oliver, J.N., "The Effect of Physical Conditioning Exercises and Activities on the Mental Characteristics of Educationally Sub-Normal Boys," *Brit. J. of Psych.,* 28, 155-165, 1958.

88. Palmer, Robert D., "Development of a Differentiated Handedness," *Psych. Bull.,* 62, 257-272, 1964.

89. Patterson, G.R. and Anderson, D., "Peers as Social Reinforcers," *Child Dev.,* 35, 951-960, 1964.

90. Peiper, Albrecht, *Cerebral Function in Infancy and Childhood,* New York: Consultants Bureau, 1963.

91. Plutchik, Robert and Petti, Rodger D., "Rate of Learning on a Pursuit-Rotor Task at a Constant Work-Rest Ratio with Varying Work and Rest Ratios," *Percept. & Mot. Skills,* 19, 227-231, 1964.

92. Preyer, W., Embryonic Motility and Sensitivity, Monographs of the Society for Research in Child Development (translated from German) 2, 6, 1937.

93. Rabin, H.M., The Relationship of Age, Intelligence and Sex to Motor Proficiency in Mental Defectives, *Amer. J. of Mental Deficiency,* 62:3, 507-516, 1957.

94. Rarick, G. Lawrence, *Motor Development During Infancy and Childhood,* Madison, Wisc.: College Printing & Typing Inc., 1952.

95. Rarick, G. Lawrence; Seefeldt, Vern D.; and Rapaport, Ionel F., *Physical Growth and Development in Down's Syndrome,* Department of Physical Education, Univ. of Wisconsin, Madison, Wisc.: August 1966.

96. Robbins, Melvyn Paul, "The Delacato Interpretation of Neurological Organization," *Reading Res. Quart.,* 59-77, Spring 1966.

97. Rubin-Rabson, Grace, "Studies in the Psychology of Memorizing Piano Music: II. A Comparison of Massed and Distributed Practice," *J. of Ed. Psych.,* 31, 270-282, 1940.

98. Seashore, R.H., "Work Methods: An Often Neglected Factor Underlying Individual Differences," *Psych. Rev.,* 46, 123-141, 1939.

99. Semans, Sarah, "Physical Therapy for Motor Disorders Resulting from Brain Damage," *Rehab. Lit.,* 20:4, 99-110, 1959.

100. Shaw, Marvin and Blum, J. Michael, "Group Performance as a Function of Task Difficulty and the Group's Awareness of Member Satisfaction," *J. Appl. Psych.,* 49, 151-154, 1964.

101. Shay, Clayton T., "The Progressive-Part vs. the Whole Method of Learning Motor Skills," *Res. Quart.,* 5, 62-67, 1934.

102. Siipola, Elsa M. and Hayden, Susan D., "Exploring Eidetic Imagery Among Retarded," *Percept. & Mot. Skills,* 21, 275-286, 1965.

103. Smith, I. Macfarlane, Spatial Ability, Its Educational and Social Significance, Warwick Square, London: Univ. of London Press LTD, 1964.

104. Smith, Patricia Cain and Smith, Alin W., "Ball Throwing Responses to Photographically Portrayed Targets," *J. Exp. Psych.,* 62, 223-233, 1961.

105. Smock, Charles D. and Holt, Bess Gene, "Children's Reaction to Novelty: An Experimental Study of 'Curiosity Motivation,'" *Child Dev.,* 33, 631-642, 1962.

106. Solomons, Gerald and Solomons, Hope C., "Factors Affecting Motor Performance of Four-Month-Old Infants," *Child Dev.,* 35, 1283-1296, 1964.

107. Stedman, Donald J. and Eichorn, Dorothy, "A Comparison of the Growth and Development of Institutionalized and Home Reared Mongoloids during Infancy and Early Childhood," *Amer. J. of Mental Deficiency,* 69, 391, 401, Nov., 1964.

108. Strickland, Bonnie R., "Need Approval and Motor Steadiness Under Positive and Negative Approval Conditions," *Percept. & Mot. Skills,* 20, 667-668, 1965.

109. Strickland, Bonnie R., and Jenkins, Orvin, "Simple Motor Performance Under Positive and Negative Approval Motivation," *Percept. & Mot. Skills,* 19, 559-605, 1964.

110. Strong, Clinton H., "Motivation Related to Performance of Physical Fitness Tests," *Res. Quart.,* 34, 497-507, 1963.

111. U.S. Department of Health, Education and Welfare, Public Health Service, Minimal Brain Dysfunction in Children: Terminology and Identification, Phase One of a Three-Phase Project, Monograph No. 3, Washington, D.C., 1966.

112. Vandenberg, Steven G., "Factor Analytic Studies of the Lincoln Oseretsky Test of Motor Proficiency," *Percept. & Mot. Skills,* 19, 23-41, 1964.

113. Walk, Richard D. and Gibson, Eleanor J., "A Comparative and Analytic Study of Visual Depth Perception," *Psych. Mono.,* 75:15, 519, 1961.

114. Walker, Richard N., "Measuring Masculinity and Femininity by Children's Game Choices," *Child Dev.,* 35, 961-971, 1964.

115. Wallis, Earl L. and Lozan, Gene A., *Exercises for Children,* Englewood Cliffs, New Jersey: Prentice-Hall, Inc., 1966.

116. Walters, C. Etta, "Prediction of Post-Natal Development from Foetal Activity," *Child Dev.,* 33, 801-808, 1965.

117. Washburn, Wilbur C., "The Effects of Physique and Intra-Family Tension on Self-Concepts in Adolescent Males," *J. of Consult. Psych.,* 26, 460-466, 1962.

118. Weinstein, S., "Tactile Sensitivity of the Phalanges," *Percept. & Mot. Skills,* 14, 351-354, 1962.

119. Werner, H. and Wapner, W., "Sensory-Tonic Field Theory of Perception," *J. Personal.,* 18, 88-107, 1949.

120. Willington, Anna M. and Strickland, Bonnie R., "Need for Approval and Simple Motor Performance," *Percept. & Mot. Skills,* 21, 879-884.

121. Wysocki, Boleslaw A. and Whitney, Eleanor, "Body-Image of Crippled Children as Seen in Draw-A-Person Test Behavior," *Percept. & Mot. Skills,* 21, 499-504, 1965.

122. Zegers, R.T., "Monocular Movement-Parallax Thresholds as Functions of Field Size, Field Position and Speed of Stimulus Movement," *J. Psych.,* 26, 477-498, 1948.

123. Zuckerman, John V., "Effects of Variations in Commentary Upon the Learning of Perceptual-Motor Tasks from Sound Motion Pictures," *The Amer. Psych.,* 5, 363-364, 1950.

WTS-X653